One Hundred Candles

About the Author

Doreen Gandy Wiley was born and raised in the Philippines and survived WWII in Manila during the Japanese Occupation. Harassed and bereft, she escaped death by a heartbeat during the liberation.

After the war she was repatriated to the United States. She earned a B.A. from San Jose State University in 1950 and an M.A. from Stanford in 1952. A longtime Oregon resident, she raised a family while teaching English in the public school system.

Her first collection of poems, *Sing the Day* (Miracle Publications), appeared in 1972. Three more collections followed: *Poems for Twelve Moods* (Dragon's Teeth Press, 1979), *A New Leafing, A Journey from Grief* (Celilo Publications, 1985), and *Say the Silence* (Celilo Publications, 1997).

In 1995, Strawberry Hill Press (Portland, OR) published her first novel, *Fires of Survival*, which won the National League of American Pen Women award for best historical novel in 1996.

One Hundred Candles: Christmas Memoirs, 1935-1945, describes the defining decade of her years in the Philippines. Of Spanish/English parents, her seventh through seventeenth years are challenged by the emotional upheavals of youth—divorce of her parents, abandonment in boarding school, and the trauma of Japanese Occupation during WWII.

Based on entries from her journals and her war diary, trapped for weeks in their hand-dug, backyard trench, *One Hundred Candles* describes in detail the fiery holocaust that characterized culmination of the Japanese occupation of Manila. Spiced with both humor and emotion, seasoned by her command of poetry, the memoir celebrates the implacable bond that accrues to a family under fire.

One Hundred Candles

Christmas Memoirs, 1935 - 1945

by

Doreen Gandy Wiley

INFINITY
PUBLISHING

ISBN 978-0-7414-0858-7

1. World War, 1939-1945. 2. Manila, Philippines.

Published by:
INFI∞ITY
PUBLISHING
INFINITY PUBLISHING
Toll-free (877) BUY BOOK
Local Phone (610) 941-9999
Fax (610) 941-9959
Info@buybooksontheweb.com
www.buybooksontheweb.com

Printed in the United States of America
Published December 2001

Dedication

To family and friends past and to those present and future
this book is lovingly dedicated.

Acknowledgments

The background scene for the cover was adapted from US Army Photo 162-12 showing the ruins of San Luis Terrace, Manila, Philippines. I have also included US Navy Photo 114-10 on page 202. This photograph which is entitled *The Shambles that was Manila—12 Feb. 1945* illustrates the extensive damage to the City, much of it, especially in the downtown section, the result of Japanese planted TNT explosives.

I wish to thank my husband Joe, family and many friends who steadfastly encouraged me to publish this memoir, and who especially hoped that I might cast it as a portrait of my somewhat unusual adolescence in Manila.

Special thanks go to fellow author William Rowan for creating the cover design and for his numerous productive comments along the way. Finally, I am grateful to John Harnish, Chris Master, and the rest of the staff at Infinity Publishing.com for their care and expertise.

Contents

Illustrations

RELATIONSHIPS

Don (Donald) and Jim (James) - my younger brothers
Maria Luling Wyss - my mother; second daughter of Teresa and Florencio
Luling
Bert Wyss - my stepfather
Ronald Staight - my father
Ethel and Mark Staight - my paternal grandparents
Teresa Luling - my maternal grandmother; widow of Florencio Luling. Their
children:
Teresita, eldest daughter married to Ovidio Arrieta. No
children
Florencio, eldest son married to Rosemary Dale. Children:
Patricia & Posy
Maria, second daughter; my mother
Ana (Annie) - third daughter; separated from John Florida.
Children: Johnny
Blanca - fourth daughter married to Dick McGrath. Chil-
dren: Dickie & Stephanie
José (Pepe) - youngest son married to Carmen Urmeneta.
Children: Nuria & Pepito
Lolita - fifth daughter married to Tom Chapman. Children:
Carol

Classmates:

Brent School: Margaret Morris, Grace Pope and Bonnie Sue Strachan
American School: Marcia Ivory, Liselotte Miller, Bill Hoffman, Jane Cothran,
Paul Davis, the Brooks twins & others.

Other Friends:

Keith & Hugh Boyd Casey, Georgie & Margie Thompson, Miriam Wright, Carmen Reyes, Harry Terrell, POW; John Smedley, Frank Kayatta, Pete Olwyler, Glenn Pinnell and other GIs.

Domestic Help:

Candida - amah and cook
Eluteria - house girl, Candida's niece
Fortunata - "lavandera"
Marco - garbage man and suspected guerrilla

Teachers:

Brent School - Miss Wilkie, Miss Kam, Mrs. Scott, Reverend Richardson
American School - Mrs. Richardson
Piano teachers - Madame Brimo, Solita Cuervo
Tutors - Mary Garcia

Neighbors:

Joan and Faust Camon
Ulla and Birgitta Greiffe & Friends from the Apartments.
The Sabater family
The Bosshard family

I

Manila, Philippines

I was seven-and-a-half when my mother married my stepfather in 1935, five years after she and my father were divorced. She said it took that long to get over him. And to prove it she married a man who was entirely different from my father. Bert was from Switzerland. He had come to the Philippines straight out of business school and worked for Nestlé's in Manila. *Bert* was a nickname given to him by fellow students because he refused to go by his Swiss name, which I'll not reveal because we were told never to mention it.

He adored my mother, Maria, partly, I think, because her outgoing, warm personality uplifted him; and she reacted to his steady, loyal nature like a woman who had been set adrift too long. Right after the wedding, which my two brothers, Don and Jim, and I were not allowed to attend because it was an affair for "grown-ups," we moved into an airy house on Peñafrancia Street located on a long, dirt, acacia-lined street where people from diverse cultures lived. Our house was one of eight wooden rentals painted either gray or dull green. Each house was built exactly alike and boasted a large, screened living room with huge shuttered windows that flapped down like lids. There were concrete floor basements enclosed in latticed wooden walls that served as combination garages, laundry rooms, and quarters for domestic help. Middle-class whites, and rich Filipinos were flanked at the end of Peñafrancia Street by a barrio, a small village made up of nipa huts, which housed poor Filipino families. Each house stood on stilts in the middle of a swampy field in which pigs, chickens and ducks rooted around for food. I often wondered how the crowded families managed to live in their one-room huts. Their children wandered up and down our street naked or clad mostly in soiled T-shirts and torn dresses cut straight like sleeveless chemises. They stood and stared at us. Sometimes they would get angry and shout, "White monkeys!" I don't remember trying to understand why they did this. I just figured that's the way they were. Later on, I would learn all about the evils of colonialism, which Americans were accused of even though they boasted the Philippines was only a Commonwealth to which they had promised independence in 1946.

My brothers and I had spent considerable time with Bert before the marriage. He roughhoused with us like a big brother and took us out regularly for ice cream in his 1930-model Ford. Still, the serious side of his nature took some getting used to. He, in turn, wasn't used to our bickering and whining. Don and Jim, being a year apart—ages five and six—didn't help, for they constantly fought on the floor like puppies. One of them would almost always end up crying. My mother sympathized and would add a Spanish maxim reflecting her ancestry, which translated into something like, *"A game of hands is a game played by villains."*

As the months passed, we enjoyed new aspects of Bert's lighter side. He would take us to the black shining beaches of Pasay, surrounding Manila Bay, and teach us to swim, all the while laughing and splashing water on us; and we, on him. His favorite trick was walking on the beach on his hands. The long trail of perfect handprints he left delighted me.

Our adjustments were small in light of our overall family relationship. It was clear that my mother no longer wore the two frown lines I was so used to seeing after my father's abandonment. For me, Bert and Maria became a pair, and though her emotions rode as clearly and translucently as butterfly wings, his solidarity, like the trunk of a tree, offered a balance. Many years later I was to realize that the unity between them was based on trust. Trust became the matrix for Maria's love, and the light that had been extinguished in her began to burn again. She had learned the meaning of new love through the loss in a failed relationship.

Bert had a unique, practical way of doing things. To this he added an aspect of surprise on the first Christmas we blended into a family. December in Manila is less hot and humid than it is during the rest of the year. Temperatures drop to about 65 degrees at night, cool enough to pull up a light sheet; but certainly too warm climate-wise to grow evergreen trees.

I'm taking a trip to Baguio," he told Maria a few days before the holidays. "I plan to find the best Christmas tree you've ever seen."

Maria's brown eyes lit up. "Shall I go with you?"

"No, I'll drive up and be back in less than two days," he answered, smoothing her dark head lightly.

"A surprise?"

"Yes, you'll all be quite surprised."

We watched Bert get ready. He packed a green flannel shirt and a wool coat into an old leather suitcase, which was decorated by numerous colorful travel stickers. Baguio was in the mountains of upper Luzon, the main island in the Philippines, where it was cool enough for wraps. I stood in the doorway of the bedroom and watched him snap his suitcase shut, his muscular arms enforcing the sharp click of the lock. Because he was so absorbed in packing, I could watch him unobserved. I remember thinking then that I was beginning to like having him as my father. I especially liked his curly copper-brown hair. He reminded me of Rudy Vallee, whom I adored. I treasured a 78-rpm record of Vallee's, and practically wore it out, playing it over and over on our gramophone.

Excitement grew with each hour Bert was gone. When he finally returned a night and a day later, he carried a tall Baguio pine, its branches full and far apart. Instantly the house was filled with a pungent, evergreen aroma. When my mother brought him a cup of warm cocoa, the smell of chocolate mixed with the scent of pine.

I sidled up to him as he sipped his cocoa, leaning close until I could get a good whiff of the chocolate. "Is the tree *the* surprise?" I asked.

His eyes teased when he answered. "Isn't that enough of a surprise?"

I stood up straight, afraid I had ruined everything, but was saved by Don, who jumped up from the wooden floor on which he sat cross-legged and piped, "Oh, there must be more!"

Bert shot an amused look at him, "How do you know?"

Don grinned, "Just, because . . ."

"Well, you just may be right."

Bert set his cup aside and began to nail the tree onto a stand he fashioned from two short planks of wood nailed crosswise. When we clamored around him, he told us to sit on the floor, far enough away so he could move with ease as he steadied the tree on its stand. When he was done, he looked straight at us, his amber eyes piercing, "It's time to begin."

No one moved, not even my mother who, all this time, watched by the kitchen door, which opened up into the sala or living room. A small smile played on her lips. *What next?* I wondered, as our stepfather disappeared into the bedroom and reappeared with a white cardboard box. He grinned as he held the box in front of us. "I am going to show you how we spent Christmas Eve in Switzerland when I was a boy. But you have to pay attention to what I say because we will be dealing with fire."

Fire! That caught my attention, and I quickly clasped my hands on my lap.

"Your mother and I will light the tree with these candles," he explained, lifting out several thick, white, three-inch candles. He secured a thick, pleated paper holder to each candle's base to ensure it would hold the melted wax, and then showed us how a metal clamp would firmly attach each candle and its holder to the branches. Then he invited us to line up the paper holders so they were ready when they prepared each candle. We immediately got on our knees and began to work as fast as we could.

"You must stay away from the tree while your mother and I are lighting the candles. After we have a few of them lit, we'll call each of you up, and you will get to light your own candle."

"Just one?" Jim asked.

"Yes, just one. We can't take too much time. You see, the candles will burn for about an hour and then they will all go out. It's not good if they burn too unevenly. Do you all understand?"

Three heads nodded. "There are one hundred candles, so let's begin," Bert continued, handing a lit candle to my mother and lighting another for himself.

One hundred candles, I thought to myself. One hundred! Fascinated, I fastened my eyes on my parents as they began to light one fat white wick after another, heads bent and hands steady. The glow from the candles warmed my mother's dark eyes. Every once in a while, her glance would catch his and then lower back to the task. I don't believe I breathed as I watched the lighting.

There were about twenty-five candles shining like stars against the green boughs when my stepfather looked up and said, "Jimmy, it's your turn first because you are the youngest and often have to wait."

Jim rose as if he were in a dream and walked on tiptoe, his knees still visibly smudged from afternoon play. He took the lit candle and held it gingerly in both hands, Bert's hand at his elbow. Painfully slowly he let the flame touch the unlit wick. As the flame leaped up, his face broke into a small-toothed smile. "Oh!" he breathed, his eyes wide open, as he stood back to admire it.

"Okay, Jim. Now, Donny, it's your turn."

His eyes luminously blue, Donny walked up, took the lit candle and silently kindled his candle. When certain it was lit, he hurried back to his place on the floor.

I had built up such a state of anxiety I couldn't move when Bert called me up. My hands and my legs felt like jelly. "Come, it's your turn, Doreen." I rose, bandy-legged as he took my hand and pulled me up. He put his arm around my waist and guided the tiny torch he placed in my hand. Inch by inch, I moved it forward until its flame touched my candle. The flame shot up like an apparition and I drew in a noisy breath. "There!" Bert cried, "I couldn't do better."

I stepped back and watched the flame flicker down, casting a perfectly round halo around itself. One by one by one, a hundred candles came to life, transforming the tree into flaming magic. When the lighter touched the last candle, we sighed, "Ahh," and "ohh." It was then Bert gave a satisfied laugh. "Surprised?" he asked. "Yes!" we chorused.

My mother's eyes glistened with tears. "It's absolutely the most beautiful tree I have ever seen," she breathed, while we stared trancelike at the hundred dancing lights.

Mesmerized, we gathered around Maria and Bert, who had settled down on the rattan sofa and watched the candles burn down until the first few began to sputter.

"So fleeting," my mother sighed. "We never had this kind of Christmas when I was a kid. We were always worried about having enough to eat after my father died. My mother had seven of us to raise," she said as we listened in silence.

Then, his head against our mother's knee, Don murmured, "The lights are almost all gone."

Sitting up from his perch at the end of the couch, Jim chimed in, "I'm hungry."

Mother got up as if on cue. "Let's have some flan Candida made this morning."

My mouth watering, I stood up and walked to wait by the open window behind the tree. I heard muffled voices and laughter coming up from the shadows that shrouded our front gate. I strained my eyes until I was able to make out the white T-shirts of several barrio children who stood and stared up at our magic tree. They must have been there for some time, as transfixed by the lights as we. I raised my hand in a half-wave. Their giggles cut sharply through the darkness and I saw their arms waving in return.

At that moment, my mother and Candida, our housekeeper, came in with flan, a Spanish custard, topped with caramel made with burned sugar. "What are you looking at?" my mother asked me. "Come eat your custard."

Candida walked over and handed me my bowl. Hearing the children below, she looked down and saw them. "I will tell them to go home," she snapped.

"No!" I cried. "Let them stay. They like the lights."

At that point everyone came to the window. It was my mother, who, having just told us what it was like to be poor, came up with a wonderful idea. "We have a few candles left in the box, dear," she said to Bert. "Let's let those children have them."

"May I take them down?" I asked as my stepfather picked up the box.

"Yes," Mother said. "You may all go down and give each of them a candle. We'll light them in their holders so they can see their way safely home."

Our parents gave us two candles apiece and followed us down with the box of matches. The children waited like statues in the dark. I imagined that I could hear them breathing very softly. Bert struck a match to one of the candles. The flickering glow brought out six shining brown faces, with eyes lit up like black jewels.

The first child, a boy about my age, reached out to grab the candle held out to him. I could see the dirt under his ragged fingernails. Holding fast to his light, he slipped behind the others, as one by one they came up. A little girl whose face I could not make out behind a veil of black hair held a younger brother by the hand. His nose was running down onto his chin. Another girl, of perhaps ten, came up next and waited as if she were at an altar. Her small smile seemed doll-like. It was she, who turned toward us after all had received their candles, and whispered, "Maraming salamat-po." I had never heard such an expressive *Thank you.* In procession, the children marched away into the black night, giggling and chattering. As they neared the end of the street, they broke into a run. Their candles flickered above their small ghostly forms like so many phantom lights.

II

A string of Christmases followed, lengthening like a chain of beads encircling a tree, some bright and colorful and others dim and barely remembered, like the Christmas after the first one we shared as a family. I don't even recall having had a tree. All I clearly remember is that my mother suddenly became ill and had to have an operation. I barely overheard her telling Bert that the doctor said she had a tumor beside her bladder that had to be removed. I knew what a tumor was, but had no idea what a *bladder* was. When I asked her a few days before the surgery, she explained it by pointing out that it was located down at the bottom of the tummy. "But what is it for?" I asked.

She hesitated, then answered. "Well, it's where the water we drink is stored before we go to the bathroom."

"You mean the bladder holds our pee-pee?"

Her face colored slightly. "Yes. But you mustn't worry. The doctor is very good and I'll be fine."

When her face turned from its normal ivory tones to a sickly pallor, I knew she wasn't fine. "You won't die, will you, Mummy? I would die, too, if you did."

She smiled and reached for my hand. Patting it, she said, "Of course not. But you need to be as good as you can because I will have to rest a lot after the operation."

After that, I decided I would have to eavesdrop if I was to find out what was going on. The next day I heard something else that worried me greatly. I was passing by my parent's closed bedroom door when I picked up on a conversation they were having. Because the walls stopped short about a foot and-a-half before they reached the ceiling, I could hear most of what they were saying. My mother's voice sounded teary. "But what about having a baby?"

"Your life is the most important thing in the world for me, for us. The doctor says we have to get rid of the tumor first. We have to trust him, dear."

A baby? Was there a baby in her bladder? I strained to hear more, but could only hear my mother's sobs layered over by my stepfather's soothing intonations.

I faced a terrible dilemma. I couldn't confront my mother about having a baby. She would know I had been listening when I shouldn't have. So I went to Candida and measured my words carefully. "I know ladies get fat before they have a baby, but could you tell me if the baby lives in the bladder before it is born?"

Candida had no idea what the bladder was. So after I explained it to her, she shook her head. "You must not ask questions like that. I cannot tell you just where the baby lives before it is born, but it is not in the—the bladder!"

"No? Where, then?" I persisted. Surely she must know. She was very uncomfortable. Shifting from side to side on her bare feet, she finally answered. "Here," she said, placing both hands on her abdomen. "Babies live in the stomach."

Astounded, I said, "With all the food?"

She scratched the back of her head and pushed the single braid she wore off her shoulder "No! They live in special sack. No more questions!"

Relieved, I hurried to get away from her scowl. At least now I knew the baby I thought my mother carried was not in her bladder. Since the doctor was operating near her bladder, it seemed to me the baby would probably be safe, especially if it was in its own special sack. I felt as if I knew a great secret, and

I decided I would not tell anyone, especially my younger brothers.

When we visited my mother in the hospital several days later she looked worse than ever. There were deep circles under her eyes and her face and arms were white as the bed sheet. Several tubes led to her body from hanging contraptions. She was so sleepy she could hardly speak. My brothers and I stood on tiptoe and tried to get as close to her as we could before Bert urged us to move away from the bed because our jostling would make her hurt. We drew away as if we had touched fire. "It's all right, dear, let them come close," she said to Bert. "I've missed you all so much. Come. Come here."

We got as close as we could without pushing on the bed. She held our hands and lifted her face to kiss us. "See, I'm doing fine," she said, mustering a smile that showed her teeth bigger than I remembered them.

In about a week she was back home. When I saw there were still a couple of tubes attached to her, I told myself there would be no baby. We were lucky she lived through the removal of the tumor, which we learned later had caused a bad infection. There were no antibiotics in 1937. Months of recovery were routine. Survival depended on a strong constitution, bed rest, and good nourishment. Bert did everything he could for her, and we children made her cards, picked flowering weeds, and told her what we experienced each day recited in fiction form, each of us exaggerating over the other, until she would shake her head and tell us not to fib. *Fib* was a nice word for *lie* and could be excused, so the next day we returned and entertained her with more stories.

One day during the monsoon season, I believe it was sometime around my ninth birthday in June, Mother got up from the rattan sofa on which she had lain for weeks and began to water the large ferns that hung from the front staircase. She paid no attention when Candida scolded her and told her she should go back and lie down. "I feel so well today," my mother said. "Better than I have felt in months."

From that day on she seemed to get better, although she complained to Bert that she couldn't understand why she got so tired. When the doctor came to the house to give her a check-up, the news was not good. "Your latest blood test shows you are very anemic, Maria. Your system has had to fight a battle. The tropics are no place to recover from what you have been through. You need to build up your blood. Have you thought of going abroad for a while to get away from this awful heat and humidity? Get away from everything and recover your strength?" He paused, and noticing her frown, added, "It would be temporary. Think about it. In the meantime, I'm prescribing some iron shots and some medicine that will help to build up your red blood cells."

After the doctor left no one spoke. My mind was racing. What would become of us? Would Bert go with her? Who would take care of us?

I was convinced the only way I would find out was to hang around my parent's bedroom door again. Mother had looked so sad I was sure she and Bert would be talking about it very soon, like that afternoon at siesta time.

I was right. I heard Bert first. His voice sounded heavy. "We've talked before about visiting Switzerland. This would be a good time to go. It would really be a vacation."

"But the children, what about the children!" she said, tears pushing through her voice "They're too little to be left."

"I know. It bothers me, too, but they'll survive. You might not get better for a long time if you stay here. That would be worse. Eventually, you could become an invalid."

There was silence for a moment. "Give me a little time. I need more time."

Greatly relieved I ran to tell my brothers I didn't think our parents would be leaving us any time soon. I was wrong. A few days later, Mother returned to the hospital for a transfusion.

Shortly after, plans were being made for a trip to Switzerland. None of the plans as to what to do with us satisfied my mother. Could we stay with my mother's mother Abuela Teresa? No because she was busy with her two youngest daughters, Blanca and Lolita, and, besides, she was still renting out rooms to boarders. Three extra children would be impossible for her to handle. Next, could we be left with Candida in the house and be watched over by Teresa or another member of our large family? No, that was out. Finally, the most dreaded solution of all came up when my blood father Ronnie said he would pay for us to attend Brent School, an Episcopalian school in Baguio, which had an excellent reputation.

When I heard the news I immediately ran and hid under my bed, where I stayed until I fell asleep and had to be called three times for dinner. Our mother, red-eyed, joined us at the table. I picked at my food as they explained how going to boarding school would be temporary, at the most a year. A year! Don whimpered and left the table, followed by Jim. I stayed and stared at my plate. Bert tried to cheer me up. "Now, Fifi," (his nickname for me), "it won't be long before we are home. We'll bring you a special gift from Switzerland. You just have to tell us what you want."

It was no use. I wouldn't be cheered up. That night I wet the bed; rather I soaked it. I had always been a bed-wetter, but had begun to outgrow it; that is, until the boarding school solution came up. Perhaps I thought if I got too bad with the bed-wetting, they would somehow let me stay home. That's not the way it worked. We would be leaving for Baguio just before Christmas vacation. Before enrolling in Brent School, we would spend a month in a cottage with Grandmother Teresa who made arrangements to leave her home long enough to help us get used to being in Baguio before becoming boarders. At least we had that to look forward to.

Our Ford sedan was piled high with suitcases, pillows and blankets. My brothers and I were squeezed in with our grandmother in the back seat. The trip to Baguio took all day and part of the night. The most difficult stretch of the ride were the last seventy kilometers or so, winding over the narrow, partly paved Zig-zag pass that took us higher and higher until we reached the winking lights of Baguio.

Jim had gotten carsick and was asleep when we arrived. I could hardly wait to get away from the stench and to stretch my legs. The first thing I saw was a tall bank of sweet-smelling pines swaying gently in a misty rain. Grandmother Teresa, whom Don had named *Belana,* because saying *Abuela* was not easy on his tongue, stepped out of the car and put a sweater over my shoulders. It was comforting to have her near me, especially because I knew I was her favorite grandchild. She preferred girls because they were not as rambunctious as boys.

The simple, square cottage that was to be our home for several weeks welcomed us with a fire, which Candida, who had ridden up earlier on the train, had built in the fireplace. In no time she called us to an oblong oak table and served us hot lentil soup and warm bread and butter. Shortly after dinner, my parents went to the Baguio Hotel to spend the night, where they would stay until after Christmas, before returning to Manila and boarding the ship that was to take them to Europe.

The next few days were a blur. The next thing I remember is waking up Christmas morning. There was no tree, but Mother had piled a stack of brightly wrapped presents under the front room window, which she decorated with a large wreath. My favorite present was a globe filled with snowy water, featuring a delicate Christmas scene. When I shook the globe the snow swirled majestically. I discovered more magic when I held the scene to the light and reflected bright beams into the globe. Using my imagination I could envision hundreds of candles lighting a Christmas tree by the side of a tiny cottage, which I thought looked much like the one we were in.

The morning my parents left remains in shadows. My mother's face and hands were cool when we kissed each other. She wore a heavy green coat and a hat that matched. She looked very elegant, but did not seem quite like my mother. Bert hugged us hard and whispered to me, "Be a good girl, Fifi. We'll be back before you know it."

I stood and frowned at him. Don't call me Fifi. I'm really not your girl anymore. And with that thought, I began to cry. We all ended up sniffling. Belana put her arms around the three of us and told my parents to go quickly.

III

Brent School was located on a hill. Its half dozen or so build-ings were completely hidden in the pines. Each wooden brick-faced structure seemed to spring out individually, as if it waited in ambush. A cool breeze blew, carrying the scent of evergreens.

Early one January morning of 1938, we walked with Belana to the headmaster's cottage to check in. The Reverend and his wife greeted us. He was a round man with dark thick hair, care-fully parted on the side and plastered down. His eyes were deep-set and peered straight at you. He wore a white priest's collar and a dark suit. I remember thinking he looked as if he was lord of the whole school. His wife, by contrast, had soft light brown curls that wreathed her girlish face like a halo. She held one of her two sons by the hand. I focused on her smile. The Reverend had met my parents before they left. He told us all arrangements had been made for us to settle into our dormitories right away. I was to be in the girls' dormitory, a wide wooden building paint-ed white, with green trim, boasting many windows, called Ogil-by Hall. My brothers, who held on to Belana for dear life, would be in the boys' Toddler Dormitory on the second floor above the general dining room, with about twenty-five other young boys.

I wept until I choked when Belana left me at Ogilby Hall. She assured me she would return the next day to see I was all right. Miss Wilkie, who was to be my teacher as I completed third grade and entered fourth, had to forcibly pull me away from Belana.

"Now, now, Doreen, you mustn't cry so. You'll make yourself sick, chile." Her southern accent caught my attention.

"Come down to my room and I'll make you some hot cocoa. You can meet Miss Kam, my roommate."

Miss Kam was a short, muscular, bright-eyed woman. She was very different from Miss Wilkie, who was so tall and thin that she seemed to sway like a slender tree, and whose face was not distinguished by feature or color, only by her dark blond curly hair. It wasn't long before she told me to finish my cocoa, as I was to meet my roommates and some of the older boarders. Ogilby Hall housed about thirty-five girls.

I was one of three girls, called *toddlers,* who were to share a room at the end of a long hall that ran the complete length of the second floor. Each of us had a small bed covered with a cream-colored blanket. A plain wooden desk flanked each bed, and we shared a large closet with separate shelves on which we folded our clothes in neat piles—one pile for underwear, one for blouses and skirts, one for sweaters, and so on. All our clothes were carefully marked so they wouldn't get lost in the laundry. I had a dozen pink undershirts and a dozen matching underpants, the nicest I had ever had. What a shame, I thought, to have to wear them in this place! My grandmother had knitted me a suit for dress-up. I wish I could say I liked it, but I hated its dismal burgundy color, which made me look pale and made my dishwater blond hair look drab. But because Belana had made it, I laid it gently on the shelf.

My roommates began to distract me from the despair that overwhelmed me. They were very different. Grace was about my age, nine-and-half or so. She was rosy and her hair was the color of ripened rice stalks. I couldn't understand why she acted so cheerful. Her smile was dazzling. Bonnie Sue was another story. Her eyes were so swollen her eyelids looked like welts, and her straight dark bangs were wet and stringy and stuck to her forehead. When she told us she was four-and-a-half, and then added that her mother had just died, I set my own sadness aside and helped her shelve her things. Gracie joined us and we finished

quickly. After that, we ran outside to play among the pines.
Dried old needles covered the ground, causing us to slip and
slide. We shouted and laughed, until Miss Wilkie called from a
dormitory window and told us to hurry for dinner.

The dining room was filled with long tables covered with
identical starched, white tablecloths. Eight to ten students and
teachers sat around each table. There must have been at least a
dozen tables in the large, windowed room. Each table had a head
person, from the school—a teacher, a nurse, or an administrator.
Formal manners were observed. I remember being embarrassed
that first night because Miss Kam, our head person, told me to
keep my left hand in my lap. "Oh, but in our house, we don't," I
piped.

"Well," she said aiming an overly patient look at me, "here,
we do."

"Oh," I said, thinking how useless my arm felt in my lap.

Every day I learned some new rule. After a while, I felt there
was always someone watching me. There were endless routines—a correct way to do each daily task, a place for every
thing you owned, and consequences if you didn't follow every
rule. The biggest consequence was a punishment called *woodpile.* It meant you had to carry pine logs up to two feet long,
from a big stockpile about half a mile from the dormitory.

The wood was stacked for use in the large dormitory fireplace. Boys and girls had separate woodpiles for their dormitories. The least amount of woodpile one could get—usually for
leaving a coat or sweater where it wasn't supposed to be—was
fifteen minutes. The most was three hours, such as for violating
curfew. The most I ever got in the year and some months we
were at Brent was one hour, and that was plenty. My arms
burned from being rubbed by the logs as I labored up the hill.
The first trip was not too bad, but the second or third time up the
path was true punishment. My legs ached and I gasped for
breath.

My emotional reactions changed while I was in boarding
school. I felt separate from everyone else. Sometimes I even felt

separated from myself. I almost never cried. I fell into expected routines, and as the months passed, I found they created a framework that felt reliable and made me feel secure. Whenever I thought about my parents, it was as if they existed in a separate compartment in my mind. I thought of them less and less. I even imagined they must have adopted me. Otherwise they would have cared too much to have left me.

One constant worry was my bedwetting. My teachers showed no mercy. They made me change my bed sheets, and when my mattress became soaked through the rubber sheet, I was told to drag it through the long hall and onto the sunroof. It wasn't a large mattress, but for a girl my size it was heavy. I felt like a turtle with a shell on its back. In a way, I was glad I could hide under the mattress as I dragged it to the sunroof to dry. Once on the sunroof, I often hung around and looked over the edge of the flat tin roof and watched my classmates wandering below. One time, one of the fourth graders passed by and looking up asked, "What are you doing up there?"

I thought fast. "Well, it's really nice up here."

"But what are you doing?"

"Oh, I'm just taking a sunbath."

"There's not a lot of sun today," she said, looking up at the sky. "Can I come up and join you?"

"You better not," I answered, standing up on the roof. "I'm about to come down."

As I got back into the dormitory, Gracie, who had been listening from an open window, said, "That was some lie you told."

"Not a lie," I countered, "just a fib."

"What's the difference? A fib is a lie."

I snapped, "A fib is a small lie. Not a bad one. It's not a *real* lie."

From that day on, we weren't as friendly. When Margaret arrived mid-term, I promptly made her my friend. She wasn't a goody-goody like Grace, and at first we got along very well. I loved to draw and so did she. We spent hours making paper dresses for paper dolls, which we created from our imaginations.

Then Grace got close to Margaret. I couldn't understand it, except that they were both of Scottish ancestry, Grace with her round rosy face and Margaret with her dark brows and sapphire blue eyes. My English/Spanish background didn't impress either one of them. There was also the problem of clothes. Grace had pretty dresses, soft prints and velvets, and Margaret naturally admired them. Although her own clothes were mostly cotton, she wore her dresses like a queen. My only dressy outfit was my hateful burgundy suit, so I had to stand aside and let them have their friendship unchallenged, at least for a while.

One evening after the dinner gong sounded, so you could hear it a mile away, Grace and Margaret marched off to supper, leaving me behind. They left the room lights on, expecting I would turn them off. Just as I reached for the switch, I decided I would leave the lights on, hoping they would get blamed.

At bedtime, the OD—Officer of the Day—gentle Mrs. Scot, came to our room. "Girls, I'm told lights were left on after you went to dinner tonight. Who was the last one here?"

I stared hard at Mrs. Scot's tidy white bun so I wouldn't have to look at Grace. Then I blurted, "Grace was."

Grace stared at me as if I had just turned into a snake. "You, you lie!" she cried.

"Uh-huh," I insisted, "you were last." As the words flew out of my mouth, I knew I was telling a big lie.

"Call Margaret, Mrs. Scot," Grace said. "She and I left together."

Blood sisters from Scotland stick together. Margaret nodded grimly when asked if I had been the last one in the room. And because I still liked her so much, I felt so bad I could not look at her.

Later, after I received a half-hour of woodpile, Mrs. Scott took me aside and asked me why I had lied. "Gracie is making me sick, Mrs. Scott. I wanted to get her in trouble."

Sensing I had told her the truth, she said, "I thought it might be something like that, Doreen. Why don't you try to make friends with one of the other girls? There's a new girl called

Marjorie who is coming in from China. Her parents are missionaries. They had to leave when the Japanese Army drove them out. She might need a friend."

And so I made friends with Marjorie, who was plain and wore glasses. I could be sure no one would take her away from me. Besides that, she shared clothes for her Dionne quintuplet doll. Her doll was *Yvonne* and mine was *Cecile.*

I met another student from China at a toddler dance sometime around Halloween. His name was Geoffrey. At eleven years old, he was tall and husky-voiced. I felt quite grown up dancing with him until nine o'clock when all toddlers had to go to bed. His stories about the Japanese soldiers who raided the Chinese village where his parents were missionaries frightened and fascinated me. "There will be a big war in Asia some day soon," he said, nodding wisely.

I would clearly recall his words some four years later.

Suddenly it was Christmas again. My beloved grandmother came up from Manila and once more we rented the little cottage where we had first stayed. Before school was out, I attended a service in the chapel. The choir was made up of teachers and older students. During Advent they performed for the student body, singing Christmas carols at the top of their voices. If this is how heaven is, I thought, I will be happy to go when the time comes. I don't recall ever hearing such angelic singing. I tried to mimic their booming, "Noels!" Hearing my voice blending faultlessly with theirs, I imagined I, too, could sing.

Belana let us decorate a small Baguio pine. She and Candida wrapped several presents for each of us. Don and Jim received penknives and handmade sweaters. I got a little red cart for my Dionne quintuplet doll. Then the best present of all wandered in—a black and white stray kitten that refused to leave. Belana told us we could keep her until school started again. We would have to take her with us after that and turn her lose. We simply called the cat *Kitty* and played with her constantly, until it was time to take her back to school and turn her lose, hoping that she would find food and shelter somewhere. Months later, I would see Kitty, who had turned into a sleek grown cat, jumping from the fence to the roof of the school's kitchen. I was satisfied she had not gone hungry.

Mother wrote to us at least once a month while we were in school. Her letters were always cheerful. She would repeat how much she missed us, and how she couldn't wait to return home. One time she described a girl who looked exactly like me. "I wished so much it had been you," she wrote. All I could think of was, How come you have to be looking at girls that look like me when you could be home with me by your side? It never made sense to me.

Our school regimentation went on month after month. I got used to dormitory life. I found repeating something many times made it familiar. But I never got used to some of the people who ordered my life. One of these individuals was the Reverend. Once a week we were invited to his cottage to listen to stories. For the most part, the stories were interesting. He read parts of *David Copperfield*, which I liked because I could imagine David's lot. It was far worse than anything I had ever experienced. Then one night the Reverend decided to tell us a true story, which he said had happened to him right outside his cottage door on one of the darkest nights of the year; in fact, not very long ago at all. Several toddler students leaned forward, eyes big with wonder. "What happened?" Bonnie Sue asked timidly.

Fully fired up, the Reverend answered. "Well," he began, knocking his black pipe against the fireplace and relighting it, "I was coming home from dinner when I suddenly saw a dark shadow by the side of the path. When I got near enough to see what it was, I was shocked." He stopped and stared at each of us, waiting for our response. My brother Jim volunteered, "What was it?"

"It was an old Igorot woman from the mountain village." He paused. "She was one of the headhunter tribe. Do you know how I know?" His eyes gleamed.

"How?" we chorused.

"Well, I'll tell you. As I got closer to her, I saw that she was chewing something."

At that point we sat in stunned silence and waited for him to continue. "Yes, she was eating the arm of her baby."

"No!" Bonnie Sue cried, putting her hands over her eyes. The rest of us sat like stones. "Why, why would anyone do that?" Gracie asked, her face dead white.

The Reverend slowly leaned back in his chair. "Because headhunters eat human flesh. She must have been very hungry to eat her own child, don't you think?"

Don, who had not spoken, got up and said, "Ugh!" When he was offered cocoa, he said, "No, thank you," as did all the rest of us.

We rushed to our dormitories. When I ran out into the dark, cold, and windy night, I wished I had had a broomstick so I could have flown straight through the window of our room and pulled the covers over my head. Joining a string of toddler girls, I raced up the hill to the dorm, sure the old Igorot woman herself was after us.

When I saw Don a few days later, he told me how upset he was. The older boys in the dormitory were teasing the younger ones without mercy. They had great fun scaring them at night by shrouding themselves with sheets and placing lit flashlights under their chins, turning themselves into ghouls. After the Reverend's tale of horror, Don and Jim were more terrified than ever when their older classmates frightened them. At least I didn't have to put up with that, so I tried to cheer him up by telling him I had heard our father, Ronnie, had left word that he would be up to see us soon. Surprised, Don said, "I wonder why he's coming now. He has never visited us up here before."

"I know," I said, "but I'm glad he's coming, aren't you?"

"Yes, but I can't tell him about the boys who scare us."

"Why not?"

He hesitated. I stared into his blue eyes. I had always envied his long lashes. "Well, he would think I'm a sissy."

In a few days our father picked us up in a long black Packard driven by a chauffeur. I was so excited that when Miss Wilkie reminded me to take time out to go to the bathroom before the long trip to Bauang, a beach community a day's drive away, I saw my father's car coming and said I didn't have to go. I suffered for miles, until we stopped to take a break past the winding Zigzag road to the western shores of Luzon, where the white sandy beach of Bauang greeted the shimmering China Sea.

Our visit would have been perfect had it not been for Doris, Father's secretary, who, it seemed to me acted more like his wife, commenting every minute on what we should be doing. Ronnie was single at the time. He had separated from his second wife and had sent her and their children to the States. I instantly hated Doris and sat as close to my father as I could so I wouldn't have to share him. It felt so good to have him hold my hand and call me *darling* when we waded into the warm waves.

Because Bert had taught us how to swim, we all loved the water, and it wasn't long before my brothers and I were up to our chins, dodging the breakers. We left Ronnie and Doris standing in water up to their knees. Their shouts urging us to get back closer to shore were lost in the roar of the surf.

I especially thought of Bert when I saw our father was not going to play with us. Standing on shore, he suddenly looked soft and golden. His strawberry blonde waves curled up tight on his wet head, and his pale tummy hung over his dark bathing trunks. But I put that image aside when we sat around a blue tablecloth spread on the sand and shared a picnic lunch. He told us amusing stories about his Cocker Spaniel *Scampy*. His English accent made him sound like Ronald Coleman, and although he couldn't walk on his hands like Bert, I felt he was very distinguished and quite rich, as he told us he would soon be heading the gold mining company for which he worked. Listening to his British accent made me think of Grace and Margaret's ancestral bond. "Daddy, is there any Scotch blood in our family?"

"You mean Scottish ancestry, don't you, darling?"

"Uh-huh, Scottish."

"Interesting you should ask. As a matter of fact, there is. My grandmother, your Grannie Ethel's mother, was Mary Campbell. She was from Scotland. Married my English granddad, James. You're named after him, you know," he explained, nodding toward Jim.

"That's wonderful," I cried, swallowing a mouthful of fried chicken.

Amused, Ronnie grinned widely. "Why *wonderful*, dear?" He lit a cigarette and proceeded to blow smoke slowly into the air.

"Because I can tell Grace and Margaret that I am part Scotch, too," I beamed.

"You mean Scottish," Doris chimed in.

It would make no difference in my dealings with my two dorm mates, for upon our return, a letter from Manila awaited us. "Good news," Miss Wilkie said, "your parents are back from Europe. You'll be going home soon. Probably around Easter vacation."

Easter vacation, it was. Separated for over a year from us, Bert and Maria seemed like strangers in a dream when I first saw them standing at the bottom of the large staircase in Ogilby Hall. Bert wore plain white linen pants and an open shirt. He had a big smile on his face. My mother began to climb up the stairs toward me, tears coursing down her cheeks. A big lump formed in my throat and I was not able to speak when she enfolded me in her arms. The familiar scent of Cashmere soap and her warm arms told me she was real and that I was not dreaming. "Oh, Mummy, oh, Mummy," was all I could say, my face buried against her fragrant shoulder.

I don't have any memory of leaving Brent School, only that we were a family again, riding down the Zigzag Pass in our burgundy-colored 1938 Oldsmobile, back to our home on Peñafrancia Street.

When we were greeted with happy shouts by Candida and her niece Eluteria, who had come to help her run our household, I was happier than I had been in ages. Added to that, I found my room had been redecorated. I had a new white dresser and blue, flowered curtains in my windows. The best surprise of all was the gift with which our parents welcomed us home—a fox terrier puppy we named *Sheba*. She was white with black and brown markings.

Brent School memories began to fade. We enrolled in the American School—I, in the fifth grade, and my brothers, in fourth and third. As soon as we got home after class, we would put on play clothes and ride our bikes up and down Peñafrancia with all the neighbor kids, as freely as if the rules of the boarding school had never existed. It felt good to get dirty, to allow my socks to be eaten by my Keds, and to be greeted by my mother as if I had come from heaven.

There was one influence from Brent that came to light shortly after we returned home. A medical report had been issued at our departure, which recommended we have our tonsils removed. All three of us had suffered colds, sore throats, and swollen glands while at boarding school.

It wasn't long before we were lined up in three beds in the hospital, awaiting surgery. The ether made me sick, and I awoke from the operation vomiting. My throat was so sore I couldn't talk. Mother was there, leaning over our beds with a wet cloth, mopping our foreheads and holding our heads over a basin when we threw up.

After a few hours I was able to sit up. My brothers were not so lucky. They moaned and groaned. "It hurts. It hurts!" they cried.

I felt I was ready for the ice cream that had been promised. Why didn't my tummy hurt? Suspicious, I sat up in bed and croaked, "Mummy, why are they holding their tummies?"

Our mother looked down for several seconds as she chose her words. "Don and Jim, you had to have another little operation, but the doctor said it will only hurt a few days."

Up until that day I had often wished I had been a boy, but no more. Apparently, my brothers had never been circumcised.

Brent School had recommended the surgery for hygienic reasons.

The months seemed to pass swiftly after we returned home.
There were no real wax candles on our Christmas tree that year,
but a tall pine brushed the ceiling, loaded with multi-colored
lights and many ornaments, some of which we children made,
and others brought back from Europe. Sheba thought the tree
was hers. She frolicked and knocked down ornaments.

In 1939, we left Peñafrancia Street and moved to a two-story
house on Protacio Street, which was located in the Pasay suburbs
of Manila. The house was new, and was finished in off-white
stucco, with a red-tiled roof and large, iron-barred windows.
Black and white tiles covered the first floor, which had a large
sala, a dining room, kitchen, a screened porch, plus an extra
bathroom. There were four bedrooms upstairs: one for my parents, one for my brothers to share, one for me, and a fourth
which served as a den. My room was actually an airy screened
porch. I loved it because the sun streamed in, and I could look
out into the street and see for blocks. At night, when the lights of
the nipa shacks across Protacio Street came on, I would watch
the people as they sat around their clay stoves, called *kalans,*
cooking and talking. The wood fires burned brightly, sending
fragrant smoke in through my window. Shortly after dusk, dozens of windows would slam shut, leaving the huts looking as if
no one lived in them. Candida explained to me that the barrio
people shut their windows as soon as it got dark to keep out the
Asuan, the bad spirits.

The people who lived in the barrio were poor, so I never figured out how they were able to have an orchestra that assembled
somewhere in their compound several evenings a week to play
classical music. I never bothered to ask, but assumed they must
have gathered somewhere under the stars, for I could hear them
as if they played in our front yard. I usually fell asleep listening
to their resounding renditions of symphonies and other classical
selections. One night I recognized Rachmaninoff's Prelude in C#
Minor. I had heard it many times at Ogilby Hall, played by an

older boarder by the name of Mary, who arose at dawn and practiced endlessly on the grand piano. As it had at Brent, the piece made my chest feel heavy, as if my whole body wanted to cry. The orchestra didn't affect my brothers in the same way. Don's bed was just a few feet away on the other side of a doorway that separated our bedrooms. He was more interested in relating the latest episode from his favorite series *Bomba, the Jungle Boy*. I loved to hear him droning on, and waited my turn to recount Tarzan's escapades from Edgar Rice Burrough's latest book.

On my twelfth birthday, I received a portable Emerson radio. It became such a delight I listened each night, partly shutting out the barrio orchestra. Don enjoyed it also, but Jim fell asleep so quickly he did not share in the pleasure of the stories or the music.

Had it not been for catechism lessons I would have been totally carefree at that time. Usually first communion took place before the age of eight. At twelve, I was not quite as receptive. I became as guarded with the nuns as I had been at Brent, wary of strict religious precepts being introduced into my otherwise carefree life. It seemed everything I did was a sin, venial and mortal. I couldn't understand, for example, why missing mass on Sunday was considered a mortal sin, one for which one could go to Hell. When Sister Clotilde drew a heart and peppered it with black pencil marks, symbolizing a heart marred by sin, I was convinced it must be how mine looked: I had bad thoughts. I told lies. Talked back to my mother. So even after my first communion, looking saintly in my white gown and net veil, I still felt beleaguered by sin. I could picture my heart forever peppered with black pencil marks.

Sister had an issue with my mother's divorce. She told us Mother was living in sin. Divorce was the worst kind of mortal sin. When Bert heard what Sister had said, he was furious. He threatened to confront her and pull us out of catechism class. Her emotions torn, our mother managed eventually to calm him down. Secretly, I wished he had carried out his threat. I would love to have seen Sister's face when he yelled at her.

Fortunately, I was able to share my feelings about catechism with Marcia, a friend and classmate, who lived two doors down. "Don't worry about it. Catholics can't be the only ones God listens to," she assured me.

Marcia and I became fast friends. We shared many interests—movie stars, swimming, playing badminton, and hanging around with the neighborhood boys. One family especially intrigued us. The father was an Army officer. He and his wife had two sons, twelve and fourteen, plus a daughter who was a sophomore. Marcia liked Keith, the younger boy, and I had a crush on his older brother, Hugh Boyd. Keith was always happy when we called him and his brother for a neighborhood game of Kick-the-Can. I never managed to gain Hugh's affections. He only noticed me when he disapproved of me. He'd wrinkle his brow over his wire-rimmed glasses and scowl down at me. But I didn't give up on him. When I discovered I could spy on him from the window of my parents' den, I hid behind the curtains and watched him at his desk doing his homework.

Marcia was fortunate in that she began to mature before I did. Although she was a year younger, she was able to fill out her bathing suit top. At twelve-and-a-half, I could only boast two rosy buds swelling imperceptibly on my flat chest. They hurt like crazy when something bumped into them. One day Jim deliberately collided with me. I yelled as if I had been mortally wounded. Despite being soundly scolded by our mother, he turned and snickered at me as he was being sent to his room.

Not long after, I decided to ask Candida when she thought my breasts would fill out. I found her in the kitchen, stirring a pot of chicken adobo, a Spanish stew, simmering in vinegar gravy. "How long will it be before I grow up here, like you?" I asked, patting my chest.

Her eyes steadily fixed on the pot, she sighed heavily. "Ayy, your questions—again!"

"Please," I urged, "Tell me. I don't want to wait months and months to look like Marcia."

She pursed her lips and shook her head. "I don't know how long it will take. Everyone is different. But," she gave a sudden sly smile, "it won't be forever."

"Promise?"

"Promise," she said and went back to her stirring.

MARIA AND DOREEN AT BAUANG, 1937

BERT AND MARIA IN SAN MARCO'S SQUARE,
VENICE, 1937

IV

A few months later I began to fill out my T-shirts.

That year was perhaps one of the most carefree of my life. A mediocre student at that time, I was good at team sports and spent much time after school playing basketball and field hockey. When I became a star at relay racing, there seemed to be nothing that could get in the way of having fun.

The fun ended with the arrival of polio cases throughout the city. The epidemic struck Manila hard. Mother lined us up as soon as she heard about it and sprayed our throats daily with a strong, antiseptic spray she said would help keep the germs away. It burned like fire in our throats. No one knew at the time where the disease came from, but it was suspected that it thrived in crowded places, especially around public swimming pools.

My firsthand experience with polio came when Jane, a studious, delicate-faced girl, who sat a row away from me in sixth grade, fell ill suddenly and was never to return to school. She had caught the dreaded polio. The iron lung in which she was placed after paralysis set in, could not keep her breathing. We heard the machine was designed for an adult, and Jane was too small to fit into it. Within a week, she was dead. A cold gray pall fell over our classroom.

Death. It came to life like one of the dreaded spirits in Dicken's *A Christmas Carol,* and haunted me every night. I imagined Jane's lifeless face. I envisioned her paralyzed body slipping into the iron lung, her breath strangling. As we lay in bed one night I asked Don what he would do if he were suddenly faced by death. Eagerly, he responded by telling me he would do what his storybook heroes did—brandish a sword or fire a gun. He was no help at all.

"What if you got sick like J-Jane?" I asked, stuttering over her name.

That hadn't occurred to him. "Well, Mom would take care of me, like she always does."

It was strange to hear him call Mummy *Mom,* a recent switch he had made to show he was too old to call her *Mummy* "You could still die, you know. Even if Mum-Mom took care of you," I said.

"Yes, but not probably," he said, his voice beginning to drowse with sleep.

As if Jane's death had not been enough, a baby in the barrio died a few days before Christmas. From my window I could see the family, in their one-room hut, gathered around a small white coffin. The dead infant was so tiny I could barely make out its doll-like face above the white sheet that entirely shrouded its body. The mother wept over the coffin, while other relatives ringed around her, praying their rosaries. Several children played on the floor. An old woman, who looked like the grandmother, stirred a pot on the kalan. When I called my mother to watch the scene, she put her hand on my shoulder. "They're having a wake, dear," she explained.

"What's a wake?"

"It's where the family gathers to pray for the dead person's soul."

"I can't stand to see it. Imagine, that baby, like Jane, will never grow up."

Gently, she led me to my bed, where we sat on the bedspread and talked about Jane. Tearfully, I was finally able to share my fear of death. "Death is part of life," my mother explained. "We all fear it because we don't know what to expect. Belana lost two babies out of the nine she had."

I dried my eyes on my sleeve. "She did?"

"Yes, in early 1900, they didn't have the medical knowledge they have now. They didn't even have running water in many areas of Manila. Electric lights had just replaced gas lights."

"Hmm," I murmured, beginning to feel sleepy as I leaned against my mother's shoulder, "Belana never talks about it."

"That's because she doesn't dwell on it. It's better to concentrate on the good things."

"I can't seem not to dwell on it," I said. "I think about Jane all the time."

"Then we need to talk about this more. It's not good to be a *worrywart*."

From then on, I was convinced I was a true worrywart, like a tiger with fixed stripes.

Not long after Jane died, I developed a high fever and sore throat. When I woke up one morning covered with a fine pink rash, it was a relief to hear my mother say, "Thank God, it's not polio. You have a good hard case of measles."

Because the fever persisted, and I developed a heavy chest congestion, she called Dr. Watrous. "Better send her to the hospital. She's got a bad case of measles and bronchitis. It could turn into pneumonia," he told her after examining me.

My mother objected. "I can take care of her here, Doctor."

Dr. Watrous, who was an ex-Army physician, didn't mince words. He shook his head and said, "Look, you have others in the family here. All of you could come down with this. At Santiago Hospital they'll put her in quarantine. I'll call and make arrangements."

Quarantine me? "No!" I cried, pulling the sheet up to my chin. "I won't go."

Under heavy gray brows, the doctor squinted at me through black-framed glasses. Without another word, he headed out the door, saying over his shoulder, "She'll need to stay about a week or so. Call me."

Because Bert was tied up at the insurance company for which he worked as comptroller, Mom called Ronnie and asked him to drive me to Santiago Hospital located on the outskirts of Manila, a long ride from the suburbs of Pasay.

I was still sniffling when my father arrived. "I hope you've had the measles," Mom said, rinsing her hands in a pan of antiseptic solution. "It's very contagious."

My father looked handsome in his white sharkskin business suit. When he smiled, his light blue eyes shone and his cheeks appeared rosier. "We'll soon find out," he said, approaching me with a blanket Mom handed him, in which he was to bundle me up so I wouldn't get chilled. Chilled! I was boiling with fever, and it was a humid ninety degrees. I could tell the way he hesitated when he approached the stairs that I was a fairly heavy load. I must have weighed just under a hundred pounds. He was gripping me pretty hard when he took a couple of steps down and tripped on a fragment of blanket trailing alongside his feet. Teetering this way and that, he cried, "Oh, good God!" and landed hard on his backside, his arms still glued tightly around me. When he peered down into my startled eyes, he began to laugh, a laugh that rose up from his belly. Pressed against him, I began to shift. This struck me as very funny and I joined him in loud laughter.

"Ay, Dios mío!" my mother cried, reaching down to help us up.

Still laughing, Ronnie said, "We're all right, Maria, just a bit shaken," he assured her, rewrapping me in the blanket and proceeding cautiously down the stairs to the car.

Santiago Hospital was Manila's newest and was run by Catholic nuns. My anxiety grew when I saw its massive buildings and upon entering its immaculate polished hallways, stark white walls, and rows of hospital beds. Nuns glided silently along the corridors, answering calls from patients. I hung on to my father's hand as I was pushed to my room in a wheelchair. Once there, I refused help from the young, round-faced Filipina nun, who instructed me to get out of the chair and into the snowy, starched sheets of the bed. When Ronnie lifted me gently out of the chair and placed me in the arms of the nun, I reluctantly allowed her to ease me into the high bed, which was about three feet off the floor. "You are safe with me, Doreen. Don't be afraid," she said, searching my face earnestly with her bright black eyes. "My name is Sister Clara. I am your nurse and I will take care of you."

Something about her voice calmed me down so I did not cry when my father brushed the top of my head with a hasty kiss, turned and hurried down the long, lonely hall.

The fever burned and congestion wracked my lungs during the next few days, causing me to sleep for hours at a time, and dulling my memory so I only remember mumbling to Sister Clara that I wasn't hungry and only wanted to sleep. She was always there when I opened my eyes. I could make out her blurred image as she placed cold clothes on my forehead and sang to me softly, hymns I did not recognize.

I knew I was getting better when I awoke one morning feeling more alert. Sister had brought a large pan of warm water to give me a sponge bath. The soapy sponge felt good on my naked body, but I turned my head away, feeling embarrassed. Then, rubbing my arm so gently I could scarcely feel her touch, she said, "Look, the rash is disappearing! You are getting well!"

I looked down at my breasts and stomach and could tell that my rash was definitely fading. "When can I get up?" I asked.

"Very soon. Maybe, tomorrow. Maybe, next day," she answered, beginning to pour warm rinse water all over what was left of my rash. As she did so, she sang. I felt as safe as I had ever felt, hearing her pure soprano, lilting and sweet, with songs of praise. I could understand why she could be happy working with the sick and dying.

A day later, she came with the wheelchair. "We're going for a ride, Doreen. I'm taking you to see something wonderful."

The *something wonderful* was a penned-up sow that had just borne ten bright pink piglets. The cement floor of the pen was covered with bloody straw—I knew about the afterbirth from Candida's reluctant answers to my persistent questions. In a corner, her large rump pressed against the concrete wall, the sow grunted contentedly, nuzzling her little ones, each one fastened onto a swollen nipple. My fingers twined into the opening in the wire fence enclosing the pen. I stared at the scene without speaking. "One of God's miracles," Sister commented, bringing me to attention. "He is a great and loving God. Otherwise, how does life occur in this perfect way?"

I had to agree with her; that is, until a dark thought entered my mind. "What happens to all the piglets when they grow up. They end up in a pot, don't they?"

She was not taken aback. "Yes, of course, some of them do. The Bible tells us it's all right to eat animals for food." A small crease furrowed between her eyes.

I stiffened. "That's a terrible thought. Imagine these little pigs being slaughtered so we can eat them." At that moment I vowed I would never eat pork again.

Eager to change the subject, Sister Clara said, "Life is a mystery. Do you know that in the Garden of Eden our first parents lived in harmony with all animals?"

I couldn't resist asking her, "Do you believe Heaven is a Garden of Eden?"

"Yes. Yes, I do, but we won't know until we get there."

I shrugged. Back to the same question, I thought, making the mystery of death the all-powerful answer to life. Sister gave me a placating glance, walked to the gate, and unlatching it, motioned for me to join her in the pigpen. As we walked towards the nursery in the straw, the sow quickly rose and stood between us and her brood, and warned us with deep, low grunts. Very cautiously, Sister put her hand on the mother pig's head and made a shushing sound. Gingerly, she moved towards the straw, slowly motioning for me to follow. When I joined her, she had already picked up one of the piglets and was holding its muggy, squealing face up to hers. "Here," she said, handing it to me.

"Wait," I cried before reaching out, "can pigs get the measles?"

She doubled over in laughter, holding the squealing pig against the starched, white bib of her habit. "Oh, my, no!"

Cuddling the piglet close, I closed my eyes and rocked for a moment. There was nothing to say.

Riding back to the hospital, I told myself that I'd remember this day always, images of the piglets rolling in a colorful film strip in my mind, their perfect pink bodies, their funny faces staring up at me, their vulnerable squeals still ringing in my ears; and on top of that, I had Sister Clara's assurance that God was in charge, whether or not I thought he should have kept us in the dark about death. Best of all, I knew I would soon be home.

V

I can't remember just when I left my childhood and entered my youth. Perhaps it was the year that Jane died, when I began to consider mortality. Perhaps it was at thirteen in 1940, when Mom—like Don, I no longer called her Mummy—allowed me to cut off my braids and get a permanent wave. The process lasted for a good five hours. I had seen my mother have a wave before, but I had never experienced it myself. I found the beautician took forever to wind my hair onto countless thick iron rods that were attached to electrical cords designed to *cook* my thin straight strands. Each wound curl was soaked in ammonia, making tears sting my eyes. I went into sneezing spasms and was told to hold perfectly still because the electricity was on, and I didn't want to be electrocuted, did I? When my curls started to steam, Fely, the operator, who was telling us her life story, suddenly cried, "Uh-Oh! Better test one before it burns!" I suddenly had visions of ending up completely bald. As she unwound the steaming rod, I watched her, fearing that she had become my executioner; then seeing her relax, I settled back down in my seat and shifted my eyes between her and the clock.

About two hours later, after all the curls were unwound, washed, and rinsed with a special solution, and washed again, I stared into the large mirror at my curly-top and decided that I would never again have to have another permanent.

My perm loosened up so that I looked very grown-up when we celebrated Belana's sixty-second birthday at her house on

Mabini Street, where she lived with two of her grown children. I can't recall a time when Belana didn't have someone in her family sharing her small rental house. It was as if her personality was made whole by the presence of one or more of her children. Somewhat like *the old woman in the shoe.*

They were all there to celebrate her birthday that April: Tito, his wife, Rosemary and their two daughters; Teresita married to Ovidio; Maria with Bert and the three of us children; Annie, who was separated from her husband, with her young son; plus Blanca and Dick and their two children; Pepe, still unmarried; and Lolita, with her husband, Tommy and their daughter.

We all mixed and blended like bread dough. Amidst the chatter of Spanish and English, we feasted on large platters of *Arroz a la Valenciana,* seafood, steamed vegetables, and perfectly caramelized flan.

Surrounded by her brood, my grandmother held court. I watched her talking to this one and that, nodding and smiling, and thought, how much my mother looked like her—the same smooth, ivory skin, deep dark eyes and hair, aquiline features, and lean body. In fact, my aunts all favored her. I didn't realize it then, but tragic as Belana's life had been after her husband Florencio died from cancer some fifteen years before, she had never lost her optimism. She perfected her sewing skills and worked as a seamstress, fashioning stylish wardrobes for the same women with whom she had hobnobbed in Manila society before necessity forced her to raise seven children by herself.

Belana's most difficult challenge was to learn to overcome her pride. Having been raised in Spain by privileged parents— her father was a general in the Army—she was unprepared to face sudden poverty. She could sew. That was the only skill she knew, by which she could earn a living.

Florencio and she were married in 1900. She traveled to Manila to begin her life as the wife of a successful businessman. In 1896 his parents had set him up with enough capital so he could go into partnership in a firm that manufactured tobacco products.

They lived well for eight of the sixteen years they were married. Then in 1906, he took an extended trip to Spain with Belana and their two children, Tito and Teresita. He left his business interests in the hands of partners whom he trusted. When he returned, he found they had squandered his share of the investment. There was nothing for him to do but find other employment. In those days Manila was a boomtown, where fortunes were made one day and lost the next.

According to Belana, Florencio found work as a customs official. All went fairly well financially, but emotionally he had been devastated by the loss of his business, and he began to drink. Once when I asked her what finally happened to him, she explained, "His heart was broken. He started to drink too much. Then his health began to go. He had a very bad cough. We didn't know it, but it was the beginning of throat cancer. He returned to Spain for surgery. He died soon after, in his mother's arms."

She took up her crochet needle and began to work on a square for a bedspread she was making. "It was those Cuban cigars he smoked constantly—I'm sure they caused it."

She didn't seem to mind my questions. I continued, "Did he lose his job when he got sick?"

"No. He lost it for other reasons and was almost sent to jail."

"Really?"

She looked up from her work. "He was drunk one night when a ship from China failed customs' inspection. He was in charge. The ship had opium smuggled on board. He was blamed, naturally."

I sank deeper into her living room sofa. She looked back down at her crochet and went on. She seemed far away when she said, "He was arrested. You can imagine . . ."

"Did he go to jail?"

"No. I was able to meet the terms of his bail—two thousand pesos."

I couldn't say anything. I waited for her to go on with a story she must have told many times, but had never gotten used to.

"We had wonderful friends. They put up the money, so he did not go to jail. But by then he was a broken and a very sick man."

"I'm sorry," I muttered.

"I know. It's a long time ago, hijita. The surgeons did everything they could, but the cancer in his larynx had spread to his vocal chords—everywhere. It was too late."

All I could think of was how unfair it was for him to lose his voice. From what Mom had told me he loved to sing. He was very smart and could speak seven languages, including Chinese.

I looked into my grandmother's misting eyes. "I'm glad you didn't die," I said.

She smiled then, and I got up and patted her shoulder. We didn't hug one another in our family; we patted and voiced quiet consolation. "Remember this," my grandmother sighed, "God gives us strength in times of need—strength we don't even know we have."

I went home that day feeling proud of my grandmother.

Other than Belana, whom I had begun to call *Grandma*, because it seemed more grown up, the other female relative who influenced me most while I was growing up was Aunt Teresita, who worked as manager of Helen's Flower Shop in the downtown district of Ermita. I enjoyed spending afternoons at the shop after my piano lessons at the music academy, which was only walking distance away. There was always something for me to do at Helen's—wash pots, help to arrange flowers, build little rock gardens, and my favorite pastime, paint seasonal designs on blank gift cards. Recognizing I had a knack for painting with watercolors, my aunt allowed me to create my own designs on cards, and later, on clay pots.

Christmas, 1940, I chose to paint old-fashioned candleholders with small white burning candles set on an arrangement of holly berries. For variety I substituted poinsettias for holly berries. The cards were so well received that one day my aunt told me to take two-dozen blank cards home and paint them at my leisure. It was the first time I had earned money for work I had done. She paid me five centavos a card.

After dinner one night, I began to paint each card and lay it to dry on the wide ledge of the tall, wide dining room window, where the Christmas tree blazed its tinsel, lights, and multi-colored bulbs. I was so engrossed I didn't hear Bert come in. I looked up to see him admiring my work. He walked over and sat on the bench of the Baldwin piano he and Mom had bought for me for my thirteenth birthday. "Say, you're pretty good," he said, pointing to the row of cards. "What is Teresita paying you?"

"Oh," I shrugged, as if it didn't matter to me whether she paid me or not, "five centavos a card."

In a mock pose, he cupped his chin in his hand and scrutinized the cards as if he were determining their worth. "Do we get interest, since we share this business establishment?"

Keeping a straight face I asked, "How much?"

"Oh, how about ten percent?"

"Too much!"

He laughed aloud. "You keep it, Fifi. You earned it!" As he stood to leave, he stared at the lit tree. "Pretty, isn't it?"

"Uh-huh," I commented, blowing on a wet card, "but not as pretty as our first one."

"You remember that? The custom I grew up with was based more on how the old Swiss cantons had adorned their trees for centuries. Decorated trees in many countries in Europe originated as part of pagan winter festivals. Changes have taken place, of course, since Christian tradition took over."

He caught my interest as he often did when he shared some of his knowledge. "I always thought Christmas trees and Christmas started out together."

He shook his head. "If I believed that, I wouldn't really enjoy a decorated tree as I do."

I knew that he no longer believed in the Lutheran religion in which he was raised. Actually, he did not believe in Christianity at all. It bothered me at first, but since I had acknowledged some of my own doubts, I found I could accept his views without believing them for myself. I was glad I had not been forced by my parents to embrace one strict religious creed. It allowed me to consider other points of view.

I suppose the technique of compartmentalizing I had adopted at Brent continued to serve me. It allowed me to keep Bert and Ronnie separate in my mind. Both men disliked each other, and I never mentioned one in front of the other. When I thought about them, I kept each one separated in my mind—pigeonholing them so they never had to mix. In that way, I allowed myself to indulge in whatever thoughts I wished.

That Christmas was our last on Protacio Street. After Bert's comments about Christmas, I observed more carefully other customs, such as the hanging of white paper stars, cut and pasted on three-dimensional frames, which the Filipinos displayed on the eaves of their nipa houses. I was quick to notice that the family, which had lost a baby last year, proudly hung a large white paper star from their window. They gathered together and talked and laughed freely. The mother held a new baby in her arms, the grandmother stirred a pot on the kalan, several children played on the floor, and the father sat in the corner and smoked a black cigar.

The New Year brought significant change to our family. Mom and Bert decided that our home on Protacio Street was too expensive. When they heard from Aunt Annie that a house she and her estranged husband Johnny had lived in was once again for rent, they jumped at the opportunity to lease it. Located on Taft Avenue, alongside of the American School, the house had a lot of appeal. It was older and built entirely of wood, with large boxed windows, which closed with traditional Philippine capiz shell, sliding shutters. Laid out on one floor, the house resembled the one on Peñafrancia Street in that it stood on heavy wooden posts embedded in the ground of an unfinished basement. Wooden latticed walls surrounded the entire lower area.

We felt lucky when we learned we could rent the house. I felt at home immediately in the airy comfortable rooms, including my own, which faced the front yard. I could look out of my boxed windows, which were so tall and large I could stand in the casings and see a large mango tree from one, and a fruit-bearing bignay tree from the other. My brothers' room was next to mine, so we could talk to one another even with our doors closed, as there was an open space between the walls and ceiling of our rooms. Mom said she had been told the house was built in the early 1900s. The growth of the trees on the half-acre of ground indicated they must have been there for some thirty or forty years. Although I knew bamboo matured very quickly, it seemed to me that such a thick wall of it, a good twenty-five feet high, must have been there a long time. The six-foot stone wall that separated our property from the school was partially banked by the wall of bamboo, which added privacy to our yard.

I found out my brothers and I could climb over the stone wall to the schoolyard by using a ladder. We climbed back and forth several times a day, and were even able to have lunch at home.

DON, DOREEN, COUSIN JOHNNY, AND JIM
WITH PET DUCKS, 1941

The one thing that would have made our move ideal would have been if Marcia could still have lived next door. I missed her terribly, and as often as we could, we would visit in each other's homes or meet at the Polo Club, where dozens of classmates got together to swim, play badminton, ping-pong, and to sit around and talk. It was an easy life. My only responsibilities were to practice for my piano lessons, and do my homework.

Homework took time. Marcia and I developed a system while still in seventh grade to do our homework as soon as we got home. We concentrated on our homeroom teacher's assignment first. Mrs. Richardson loaded us up on reading in our American history book. When we were through going over our daily assignment, often an entire chapter, we had to outline the main points in special notebooks, which she checked regularly. At first the chore was overwhelming. I was often on the phone exchanging views with Marcia. Gradually, we discovered that it was fun to practice our best writing, using clear blue ink in our fountain pens, as we wrote our outlines. Mrs. Richardson beamed when we turned in our carefully penned work. We never told her that penmanship, not history, was our main interest.

Our school year began in June and ended in April. When the monsoon season hit, bringing its typhoons and hot humid weather, we were in school. The months of April and May were essentially dry for two month's of vacation. We moved to Taft Avenue as the school year ended in 1941. At that time Manila was abuzz with news of Army and Navy families leaving the islands because of the threat of war with Japan. Many of our Army and Navy classmates left on the President Coolidge. This caused concern and prompted class discussions about the exodus. We studied Japan's invasion of China in 1937, the German Army's takeover of Poland in 1939, and Japan's alliance with Germany and the Vichy Government of France. We also explored the fact that the Philippines had been building its defenses under General Douglas MacArthur since 1935, when he was appointed Field Marshall in charge of training infantry reserves and strengthening the entire Army and Navy.

It was then I recalled what Geoffrey, the student at Brent whose parents fled the Japanese in China, had said about an eventual war with Japan. Why, I wondered, why was he was so sure that war was inevitable? One day in class, I asked Mrs. Richardson.

A tiny woman who wore no makeup and who sat purposefully behind her desk, Mrs. Richardson considered my question for a few moments before responding. "Well, we've discussed the fact that Japan is overpopulated. They lack natural resources—oil, steel and other products. What would you do if you were dependent on other nations for these necessary resources?"

Wishing I hadn't opened my mouth, I slid back in my seat. I could hear laughter from the back rows where some of the mischievous boys sat. "Uh. Well, first I would try to make friends with nations that would help me."

"Good answer. What if that didn't work?"

"Then, well, then, I guess I might think about getting resources elsewhere—from countries that maybe weren't so friendly."

Pleased with my answer, she pushed further. "Might you use force if you became too desperate?"

I sat up in my seat. "Yes. Yes, but just how would the Philippines be so important?"

Hands shot up all over the room, and we were off to a lengthy discussion. Mrs. Richardson beamed as she witnessed class enthusiasm. Subsequently, she stood up and walked to the center aisle. "Good job, class. Thank you, Doreen, for your questions. Do you have your answers now?"

I felt the blood rush up to my face. Taking a deep breath and staring at Marcia for support, I said, "Yes. We have rich resources, but mostly it's because the Philippines is a military threat to Japan."

After dinner that evening I decided to check on Bert's point of view. When I reviewed the discussion that had taken place in class, he said, "Sounds like your teacher is very well informed.

She's absolutely right. It's interesting you should bring this up because I've been talking to Mom about getting away and going to the States, or to Europe with you kids."

Surprised, I asked, "Really. Do you think war might be that close?"

He had just lit a cigarette and he drew on it heavily. "Yes. When the military families leave, that tells you they know more than we do. Frankly, I'm worried."

"What does Mom think?"

At that moment Mom walked into the living room and sat on the sofa beside him. She had on her print lounging robe. Her face was slightly flushed from the humidity often felt most when night was coming on. She spoke up. "*Mom* thinks we should stay here. This is home. My whole family is in Manila. Why should we leave?"

It was one of the rare times I saw Bert become impatient with her. "You know very well *why*. All of Manila knows why. But it's easier to deny the possibility and convince yourself war is not a threat."

She shrugged her shoulders, though I could tell she was in some conflict, and then added, "I know, but what would I be doing without you in a strange country with three children? If war came and you were stuck here, I'd be frantic. You know that. We all belong together."

That ended the discussion for the time being. Bert would not leave his job in Manila. Mom was right in a way, as I saw it, but so was he. The question of war continued to nag at me as it did others. In July, back in school after vacation in April and May, we heard the Japanese had struck at Indochina. They occupied Da Nang and Saigon. President Roosevelt declared an oil embargo against Japan and froze Japanese assets in the United States.

Rumors flew in Manila. But despite the fear that war could break out in the Philippines, most everyone chose to deny the growing possibility and went on with their daily lives. Meanwhile, the shadow of war spread over the islands. As General

MacArthur tried to get increased military support from the States, we saw more American soldiers arrive and more planes in our skies—a temporary comfort.

I wanted to believe that as long as Marcia and her family weren't going anywhere, ours, too, would be safe in Manila. She and I saw each other at school daily. We were both on the basketball and field hockey teams. During free hours we met at the Polo Club and also went to movies. Our interest in boys grew. Hugh Boyd and Keith had sailed to the States in April along with hundreds of military families, but we had found other heartthrobs—older boys who had no idea how we felt about them or that we exchanged secret messages and followed them around.

On weekends, our family went on outings. We usually drove to recreation spots that had water. One of these was Ipo, a morning's ride away, where a clear green river flowed among huge smooth boulders. In the emerald clarity of the water, my brothers and I would swim underwater, imagining we were characters in a Tarzan movie. Free from the stress of work, Bert joined us in playing water tag. He was like a fish underwater, and I could never get away from him, nor could Don and Jim. Trying to outswim him became a heady challenge. I laughed to see his wavy hair plastered straight over his forehead when he surfaced. Once on shore, he would shake the water from his body like Sheba, spraying any of us who were close by. Mom, in the meantime, spread a picnic lunch on the pebbled beach and chuckled over us. It is how I remember my parents best, enjoying cool, leisurely hours in the pre-war tropical ambience of Ipo; and we kids, soaking wet, gathering around the picnic lunch, anticipating sandwiches and sweetened calamansi juice.

Back in school, Marcia and I became complacent in following the boys we had crushes on. It never occurred to us that our sneaky setup, whereby we enjoyed targeting certain heartthrobs without having to have any relationship with them, could be made known, and consequently be challenged by one of the boys. Our secret crushes on two freshman students, John Hill and Bill Hoffman, were ultimately revealed. We couldn't imagine who had told on us. We had only referred to them in code names—*Rain* and *Purple*. It never occurred to us that perhaps our behavior around them might have given us away. Once discovered we were so embarrassed we stayed completely away from them, and, in fact, hid whenever they came anywhere near us. John, who was interested in a sophomore girl, paid no attention to us; Bill was apparently flattered to know we liked him. He turned the tables on us by focusing his interest on us, and, specifically, on me.

I was caught in such a dilemma I thought about quitting school. I couldn't possibly return his attention. My loyalty to Marcia was far more important. How were we to share him? Impossible. And yet, I did like him, a little . . . I had no choice: Caught in an emotional web, I had to pretend I wasn't interested in him.

Pressure from having to carry on this act was eased when our seventh and eighth grade basketball team was invited to play against Brent School in an all-school competition. I concentrated my efforts into getting ready for the tournament, which was scheduled in late November. I was excited as I packed for the weekend train trip to Baguio. I can't remember much else that happened until I was actually on the old train, its iron steam locomotive pulling five or six cars filled with students from the American School. My ears rang from the voices of classmates, competing with the train's chug-a-chugging as we rattled over miles and miles of rail that cut through rice fields, and seemed to extend beyond the horizon. Hundreds of Filipino families tended the fields, bent over the furrows, while others labored on foot behind primitive plows pulled by lumbering carabaos. Young children played close to their parents, while their older siblings worked in the fields. The countryside was dotted with barrios, around which grew groves of coconut and banana trees. Lush tropical greenery predominated except for the distant mountains that rose like purple velvet to meet the bright spill of the sun.

The cars were fashioned with windows that could be lowered. It was not long before every window in our compartment was down, letting in coal smoke along with the heat of the day. Our mood was high. We began to mill around, chattering and laughing shrilly, finally exhausting ourselves long enough to stop to eat sandwich lunches from home. Marcia and I sat together, but I found my attention focused on Bill who made sure he walked through our car periodically. As he went by our seat, he quickly looked my way and shot a smile at me. Once or twice he merely passed by and raised his eyebrows. Each time, Marcia would poke me in the ribs with her elbow and whisper, "There he comes again. He must really like you!"

What was I to do? I decided to face straight ahead, shifting my eyes so I could see him go by. I was no longer play-acting at romance. I had suddenly become a player, reluctant and inexperienced, perhaps, but a player.

When we arrived at the familiar Baguio Hotel, I looked around its rambling, old compound made up of one large wooden unit and several cottages laid out on a large piece of land, which was meticulously landscaped with tall pines and flowering bushes. The furniture in the lobby was traditional, and was accented by flowered cushions, which were laid out on comfortable sofas and rattan lounge chairs. It seemed a long time since we were here with Mom and Bert before their trip to Europe.

I joined three of our teammates in a room with two bunk beds. The first thing we did was to get our uniforms ready for the game the next morning. The second thing was to hang up our formal gowns so they would not get more wrinkled before we ironed them for the dance.

There were several games played by teams from both schools. Looking around, I was only able to recognize and wave to a few students I remembered from Brent. As I sat waiting with our team, I found my stomach tightening and my breath becoming shallow. "I'm not up to playing today," I whispered to Marcia, sitting next to me. Mary, one of our best forwards, heard me, and sticking her head between Marcia and me, hissed, "You've got to play well. We've got to beat them!"

After Mary settled back down on the bench, Marcia gave my hand a squeeze. "Are you worried about what Bill will think?"

As was so often the case, she targeted my fear. I caught my breath as I answered. "Yeah. I think so."

"Pay no attention to him," she said in her no-nonsense manner.

I wish I could say her advice helped. I played poorly. In fact, I made a fool of myself. I missed a basket as it sailed over my head and out of bounds, with me teetering backwards and sliding on my fanny to an abrupt stop. I heard a collective moan from our bleachers. Our opponents grabbed the ball and went for a basket. I was relieved when I was benched. I could hardly face my teammates in the locker room, despite the fact that we did win the game.

My teammates were still chilly when we returned to the hotel, and they didn't begin to warm up until that evening when several of them admired me in my new formal gown. It was cut in princess fashion to several inches below the waist, and then flared into a cloud of blue organdy, stitched with tiny pink embroidered flowers. The scooped neck and slightly puffed sleeves added to its classic style, and I suddenly felt like Cinderella. Not only was I relieved that my teammates forgot about my blunder, but I found a growing excitement that Bill would be at the dance. I felt sure he would ask me for a dance.

As I entered with a crowd of girls, I spotted him across the ballroom. He was dressed in light tan slacks and a dark tan blazer. His black hair was carefully parted and combed, and his eyes brightened when he saw me. He not only asked me to dance once, he was at my side the entire evening. When we danced to several slow, cheek-to-cheek numbers, I could feel his breath on my forehead, and I detected a scent of fresh soap. Every once in a while, I caught Marcia scrutinizing us as she danced with boys from our class. When she passed by once too often, I scowled. She gave me an arch grin in return.

After several numbers, I worked up the nerve to ask Bill what he thought about the games. First, he mentioned the freshman competition in which he had played; then he said, "You guys did fine. You won."

I looked up at him to see if I could read anything further from his comment. "No thanks to me. Did you see me lose the ball and flop down like a fish?"

He grinned. "Yeah. That can happen. You did O.K."

"I did?"

"Sure."

"You watched me?"

"Sure."

He made my evening. The dance ended abruptly at 10 P.M. for everyone but the high school teams, who got to stay up until midnight. When we returned to our room, my roommates, including Marcia, teased me for spending all my time with an upperclassman. I didn't care. I knew it was friendly teasing.

Riding back to Manila on the train I made sure I stayed with my team, once again pretending to ignore Bill's attention as he walked through our car. By the look on his face, I knew he sensed what I was up to. Marcia knew, too, when she looked at me and fixed her keenest expression on me. "Don't lie and tell me you don't like him."

"Not even a fib?"

"Not even."

VI

Exactly one week after we returned from Baguio, the Japanese bombed Pearl Harbor. Within hours, Japanese warplanes approached the Luzon coast on their way to bomb Camp John Hay in Baguio, killing several civilians and wounding dozens of others.

I heard the news while our family attended Uncle Pepe and Aunt Carmen's wedding at the San Marcelino Church on December 8, the Feast of the Immaculate Conception. The news exploded at the back of the church just as my uncle lifted the veil over his bride's face and kissed her. Serpentine words, "Japs bombed Pearl Harbor!" snaked from one pew to the next, until the whole church was caught up in a crescendo of emotion, including the bride and groom, who stood at the altar, stunned.

Dressed in embroidered white robes, Father Monaghan motioned for us to quiet down. I'll never forget how his resonant Irish voice wavered and how his face became bright red as he spoke. "Be calm, everyone, please. No need to panic." He paused, and then asked, "Here, here, who brought this terrible news?"

Dozens of heads swiveled towards the back of the church. One of the wedding guests rushed up the aisle and blurted, "Father, it was Mr. Santos, a friend, who stopped by to say he had just heard it on the radio." Out of breath, he added, "The Japs have also bombed Camp John Hay in Baguio. A woman lost her leg. Nine others were killed or wounded!"

Father began to wave his arms. "Thank you. Thank you. Stay calm now, everyone," he cried, his voice beginning to boom. "Go quietly to your cars. Go home where you will be safe." Then almost as an afterthought, he turned to the bride and groom and raised his hands to bless Pepe and Carmen, who were wrapped in each other's arms.

Mom put her hand on my shoulder, "Wait until the crowd thins out. We'll congratulate Pepe and Carmen, then leave. Don't hurry."

I looked over to check on my grandmother, Aunt Annie, and cousin Johnny, who were sitting motionless in a pew across the aisle. Minutes before, Grandma had watched her youngest son and his bride get married. She had looked proud in a beige gown with a lace collar she had fashioned especially for the wedding. Aunt Annie, in a bright blue print, had looked happier than I had seen her since her separation from her husband, and my seven-year-old cousin had waved to me.

Just as we rose to file out of our pew, Don cried, "Something is wrong with Jim!"

Our younger brother lay in a heap on the floor, his head resting on the wooden kneeler, his eyes shut. He was as white as the marble pillars of the church. I stared at him and felt my stomach lurch. Without a word, Mom and Bert lifted him onto the wooden seat, unbuttoned his white shirt, and fanned his face with the wedding program. Uncle Tito hurried over with a wet handkerchief, which I suspect he must have dipped in the holy water. As soon as Mom put the cool, wet cloth on Jim's forehead, his eyelids quivered and his eyes opened. "You're all right, Jimmy," Bert said, putting his arm firmly around him and easing him into a semi-sitting position.

"I feel sick," Jim muttered, pressing his face into Bert's chest. "Burning up."

Mom leaned over and brushed her lips over his forehead. "Fever. We need to get him home."

The church had turned into a madhouse. Pepe and Carmen looked wilted in their wedding attire, he, in a white tuxedo jacket with matching black trousers, and she, in a flowing tulle gown that enhanced her Spanish features. They were being pressed right and left by family and friends who offered hasty congratulations and farewells.

I felt sorry for them. Minutes before the news broke, soft organ music, dozens of lit candles, and the scent of roses had surrounded them. Now, for them, for us all, one word resonated over the gold-leaf arches of San Marcelino—War!

Twenty-four members of our family retreated to their cars. The bridal couple rushed off to her mother and father's home to decide what to do. They had planned to travel in the southern islands for their honeymoon. Travel was out of the question now.

When we got home, Bert immediately clicked on our radio—a Philco upright that sat in our living room. We glued ourselves around it, except for Jim, who lay listless on the sofa, an ice bag on his forehead. We heard President Roosevelt's speech on the shortwave band, declaring war against Japan and citing details of the Japanese sneak attack on Pearl Harbor, calling it, "A day that will live in infamy." That wasn't all. There was news that eighty Japanese warships had been sighted at Aparri, off the northernmost coast of Luzon. More ships were reported off Lingayen Gulf to the west, near Bauang beach, and landings were expected at Vigan and Ilocos Sur. Davao, on the island of Mindanao, had also been bombed.

"Goddammit!" Bert cried out, "They're surrounding us—north, south, east and west!"

My head whirled. This is a nightmare. All the scary talk of war over the last few months was just that—talk; now, the sudden reality—impossible to accept. I had never quite understood the meaning of *shock,* as I did at that moment. I'll call Marcia, I told myself, she will relate to the news as I have. I dialed her number and was relieved to hear her breathy voice. "My God, Marsh," I blurted, "isn't it horrible?"

"I'm sick. Just sick. School's closed, you know. We're sitting here by the radio. It's getting worse by the minute."

"School is closed? Christmas vacation hasn't started," I said.

"They sent us home at noon, Doreen, while you were at church. We can't go back until they tell us." She paused. "My Dad says we won't be going back soon."

"What do you mean?" I asked, aware that she was in as much shock as I.

"He says that if the Japs land, we'll be at war for weeks before we beat them."

I could feel a lump growing in my throat. I couldn't respond. "Doreen?"

"I'm here. Uh, I just don't know what else to say, Marsh."

"It's just so awful. I'll call as soon as I hear more. Or if you do, call me."

I stood by the telephone, collecting myself before rejoining the family. I looked over at Jim. He was dozing, still burning with fever. Mom said she was sure he had a case of *dengue,* a flu-like illness that struck most everyone in the islands at one time or another. The symptoms included high fever and severe muscle aches, mostly in the neck and back. Because of this, dengue was called *back-break fever.*

Bert suddenly turned off the radio. "We've heard enough for now," he announced. "We've got to plan what we're going to do when we get bombed."

"You mean they'll bomb—like tonight?" Don asked, his eyes wide with disbelief.

"Yes. That soon, I think. Jap planes are within range from their ships." He took a sip of iced water from the rattan side table. "We have no shelter yet, but we can go to the stone wall in back and crouch down for protection. O.K.?"

"O.K.," we chorused. Mom spoke up. "We need to protect ourselves against concussion. I've gathered up some pencils to put between our teeth to keep our ear canals open when the bombs blast."

Mom had taken a Red Cross first aid class in recent months. Concussion was something I didn't know much about. "What happens if we don't?" I asked.

"You could become deaf," she explained. "Keeping your mouth open keeps the passages free and the pressure from building."

We would gather around the radio many times in the next few days, but for the time being, we ate a quick dinner of cold cuts and fruit, which Candida and Mom prepared, and then went to bed.

At 3:30 A.M. on December ninth, just hours after we had gone to sleep, we heard the air raid siren's reverberating whine. We leaped out of our beds, and ran down to the stone wall. Bert carried Jim, while the rest of us lined up quickly against the wall. In a matter of minutes we heard the drone of Japanese bombers, and a rain of bombs began to fall. Nichols Field, three miles south of us, and other targets in Manila were hit repeatedly by several waves of aircraft, which sounded like giant bees. I bit my pencil so hard I gave myself a headache. The bomb blasts cracked the air and shook the earth on which we crouched. I counted the heavy thuds—*crrr-ump, crrr-ump*—until I lost count. The sky was ablaze with antiaircraft. It streaked like orange fireworks as it *ack-acked* overhead. Rounds of flares went up. We learned later that saboteurs set them off to help the Japanese find their targets. Traitors!

I glanced at Bert's set face and could see his eyes reflecting intermittent glints from the antiaircraft shell blasts. Mom had one arm around Jim and the other wrapped tightly around Bert's waist. Candida and Eluteria held each other, while Don tried to calm Sheba who was barking furiously.

When the *all clear* blasted, we trudged back up to bed. Mom told us at breakfast that she had not slept much, but I was so exhausted from the shock of the last twenty-four hours, I slept as if I had died.

Before lunch, Bert gathered shovels, picks and hoes and we began to dig an air raid shelter in a site a few feet from the stone wall that had protected us hours before. As the Japanese landed on Luzon at Aparri, Lingayen, Vigan and Legaspi, we dug a trench shaped like an L; the short end was three feet long, and the long end was twelve feet in length. Both ends were open. The short end was the entrance. The long end was five feet in depth so we could walk into the shelter in a fairly upright position. Bert designed the roof of sturdy planks, which rested on four-by-four supportive posts dug into the ground. Sandbags would cover the roof, finally packed by a deep layer of earth on which we would plant camote, a dense sweet potato vine, for camouflage.

In between air raids we dug like we were on a schedule. We were like the seven dwarfs carrying their picks, shovels, and hoes in the recent *Snow White* movie, one of the first Technicolor films produced. I wish I could say I was enthusiastic about the work. I hated the dirt that accumulated under my fingernails as I packed it on the sides of the trench. My nails cracked and my fingers were rubbed raw. But there was no doubt that, despite the hardship and inconvenience, we were joined in a family effort which would add to our safety during air raids, as well as in battle, should it come to that. For that, I was grateful. I put up with being teased for being persnickety. Even Jim, who was getting over dengue fever, proved to be hardier than I, so I couldn't complain too much at having earned the nickname *Queenie.*

On December 10, just as we got started digging the shelter, we had an interruption that brought unexpected brightness to our war-clouded lives. After we had cleaned up sometime in mid-afternoon, we heard calls from our eight-foot, iron-barred front gate, which led into the compound we shared with the neighboring Camon residence. "American soldiers!" yelled the boys, who ran ahead of us to open the main and secondary gates that led into our driveway. The four soldiers standing there were a real sight. Their olive-drab fatigues and boots were covered with mud, some of it still wet. Their faces were smeared with dirt and perspiration. They carried rifles and helmets and looked as if they had not rested in days.

One of the men stepped forward and extended his hand to Bert and then withdrew it. Smiling apologetically, he said, "Sorry sir, I'm too filthy to shake hands. Second-Lieutenant Ross here, and these are my men from the Third Pursuit Squadron. We drove from Iba, Zambales."

By then we had formed a ring around them. Bert nodded a greeting and quickly motioned them forward. "Come in. Come in, please. How can we help?"

As we walked together to the house, Ross explained what had happened. "Japs caught our P-40s refueling after we'd raided them this morning. They wiped us out. Same thing happened at Clark Air Force base. They got our B-17s there." He breathed heavily for a moment. "We're trying to locate our C.O. He lives on Taft Avenue, somewhere around here."

"Iba!" Bert said, "my God, that's about one-hundred-fifty miles from here."

"All we want is a drink of water, sir, and time to take a short rest before we go on."

"Sure. Sure." Bert waved them up the back steps through the hallway by the kitchen, where they laid their rifles and helmets on newspapers.

Mom hurried alongside the officer, "You can take showers if you like. Clean up a bit. We'll fix something to eat."

It was at that moment that I sensed one of the soldiers was staring at me. Without turning my head, I shifted my eyes and caught his face as if I had framed it in a camera lens. My heart tripped as I met his eyes. They were the most intense blue I had ever seen, and brightened by a smile that began from a row of white, even teeth. His hair was light gold, streaked with dirt here and there, and wavy. In the muddy fatigues he wore, his body looked lean and slim-waisted. "Hi," he said directly to me, "I'm Harry."

I turned shyly and returned his smile just as all the men began to introduce themselves. I was so struck by Harry I couldn't remember all their names. One was from Brooklyn, the other was from the South, and Second-Lieutenant Ross was from the Midwest, I believe.

It wasn't long before they decided to take showers, two in our upstairs bathroom, and the other two in the basement shower.

They put their dirty uniforms back on, but their faces looked several shades whiter when they came into the dining room in their stocking feet. I could tell by their smiles how pleased they were to see the ham sandwiches and calamansi juice that Mom, Candida and I had laid out. I had eyes only for Harry. As he helped himself to a couple of sandwiches, he said, "It sure feels good to be clean, even in these," he pointed to his stained, mud-caked fatigues. "Still a mess from the bath I took with a carabao."

His comment got everyone's attention. "With a carabao?" Don questioned.

When Harry grinned, I noticed again how his whole face lit up. "The raid caught us by surprise. We scrambled for cover. I found a carabao mud hole in a nearby field and jumped in. You should have seen how he sloshed around trying to get rid of me."

We all laughed. I was glad I wasn't the only one looking at him. I lowered my eyes to force myself not to stare. Soon we were all chattering. As usual, war talk predominated. Ross shook his head over the losses suffered at Iba. "Damned Japs destroyed our main force. A lot of those P-40s just arrived in the last few weeks."

Chewing on a mouthful of sandwich, Don asked, "Are you guys pilots?"

"No, ground crew. Radio operators," Ross explained. "Lost a lot of men in that raid. Clark Field did too."

Bert shook his head. "Iba and Clark are our main air defense."

"Yes, sir, they are."

"Looks bad. The Japs are advancing."

"Don't like to say it," Ross said, "but once they've landed, we can't stop them without air power."

An uncomfortable silence followed, which was broken by Harry who began to tell Mom about himself. He was from Colorado, and had two brothers younger than himself. I found myself blushing as I concentrated on his animated face. He reminded me of William Holden, a rising Hollywood star, and I was secretly pleased when he said his outfit was scheduled to spend ten days at a converted rest camp at La Salle College, just down the street from our house.

When the four of them left about an hour later, they thanked us again and shook hands with each of us. I felt Harry's strong fingers and noticed his broad wrist as he held my hand an extra second or two. A strange electric-like charge raced through me. "When I find out our schedule at the rest camp," he said, "I'll see if I can take some time to come back to say 'hello' to you all."

I didn't know how to respond. "Oh, yes," Mom smiled at him, "come back anytime. Come back, all of you!"

I felt the blood thumping in my ears as we waved to them at the gate. "What's wrong with you?" Don asked, cocking his head. "You look funny."

I shrugged. "Nothing!" I snapped. Out of the corner of my eye I saw Mom staring at me. She was wearing a half-smile.

For the next few days, I was restless with anticipation. Then on December nineteenth, as we were getting ready to begin work on the roof of the shelter, we heard someone whistling at the gate. "It's Harry!" Don cried, running to open the gates, with Mom, Jim and me following. We greeted him like he was a lost relative. Handshakes and smiles all around, and it wasn't long before he agreed to join us for lunch. He mentioned he had been involved in activities at rest camp and now had a day's leave before his outfit was scheduled to leave Manila.

"Where will you go?" I tried not to show my disappointment. As the Japanese bore down on us, hundreds of trucks had been rumbling by every day transporting the armed forces in a retreat out of the city.

He cleared his throat. His voice was deep and resonant when he answered, "Don't know for sure, but scuttlebutt has it that we'll head for Bataan."

At that moment Bert appeared. He had just come in from a trip to his office, where business had ceased during the emergency, but where many of the employees returned to take care of essential matters as the crisis grew. "Hi, Harry. Nice to see you again. I just heard your comment. It's obvious our forces are on the retreat. Bataan is part of *War Plan Orange,* isn't it?" he said, referring to a strategy the newspapers explained, which he had discussed with us. The plan had been designed by the armed forces and the Philippine Commonwealth in 1924. It spelled out a retreat to the Bataan Peninsula, some eighty or ninety miles from Manila, where Philippine/American Forces could mobilize a defense, with the support of Corregidor, an adjacent island fortress in Manila Bay. Concentrating our defense in this manner would hold the islands until reinforcements arrived from the United States.

It was obvious Harry couldn't say too much. He nodded his head. "Yes. Bataan is part of the plan. But, listen. Don't worry. Reinforcements will arrive. When we get some air support, we'll let them have it."

Bert looked askance at Mom. She frowned in return. "Hope you're right, Harry," he said.

No one responded. We wanted to believe a counter-offensive would happen right away, but in the meantime, the specter of a huge Japanese Army descending on Manila spread a black shadow on our hopes. Harry sensed our mood and tried to lighten it. "I'm sure glad we could visit again," he said.

"Here, let's bring the lawn chairs around and have that visit," Mom said as she arranged the chairs in an informal circle, making sure Harry was in the center. We visited over iced calamansi juice. Mom and Bert went upstairs after awhile, and Harry was left with the three of us. He told us he liked to draw. Did we have some paper and pencils? Don and I dashed upstairs and brought back the items he requested. I threw in a charcoal pencil and some lined paper. For the next hour Harry displayed his artistic talent by entertaining us with his drawings. He sketched scenes depicting his Colorado background and his Army life, plus added some imaginary scenes. In one sketch he pictured a skunk trailing a skier; in another, he drew an officer he said was his C.O., purposely exaggerating his appearance; and in another, he sketched a large Spanish galleon tossing on a turbulent sea.

When he tired of that, he drew cartoon-like animal faces, including the head of a puppy that was pouting. He looked up at me and said, "That's you, Doreen."

"No!" I cried, faking an objection. Having sat in the sun watching his hand move magically, I found I was beginning to relax, almost as if I had known him for a long time.

"Hey," he leaned forward, "hold still, let me draw you."

Flattered beyond anything I could say, I sat perfectly quiet while he drew my profile. I knew I was blushing again, but he didn't act as if he had noticed it. When he was finished, he said, "Here. It's not as beautiful as you, but it'll do."

Beautiful? He could have sketched an old crone and it would have been all right with me. "Do I pout like that, really?"

"Sort of."

Don, who was restless, watching me get all the attention, perked up. "She pouts when she can't get her way."

Jim was quick to chime in. "Yeah."

"Aw, come on," Harry said. "You're all great." He told us then we reminded him of his family. When he mentioned his brothers, I asked, "No sisters?"

"No, but if I had one, I'd like one just like you."

It wasn't exactly what I wanted to hear, but it was fine because he said it. He talked on and on, telling us about himself. He was twenty-three years old and had left home after attending commercial art school to join the Army. When we asked him why, he explained that he had some trouble with his folks and wanted to get away for a while to see the world. His voice dropped when he added, "I'm sorry I did that. Wish I were home and not stuck out here. I just had a few months to go before finishing my hitch and returning to the States."

He didn't seem to want the afternoon to end anymore than we did. He took up my lined notebook paper and we went up to the living room, where he turned on the radio and began to decode radio messages in Morse code. Fascinated, we watched and listened as he explained his job as a radioman. His writing was flowing and clear and seemed a reflection of his personality. I

had never experienced the feeling I recognized later as budding
love. I knew how I had felt about Bill, but my reactions paled
when measured with what I felt for Harry, this young soldier
who had walked into my life, who drew magically, and smiled in
a way that made my heart sing.

When he left, the sun was beginning to set, casting long rays
on his uniform and creating a halo around his wavy hair. He took
away the brightest moments we had experienced, in a time when
the future looked like an abyss, and when Christmas would have
little meaning—no tree, no candles, no gifts—a bleak 1942, just
days ahead.

While he was taking a walk around the yard, Bert found me
a couple of days later in my hiding place behind a multiple-trunk
bonga betel palm, which grew twenty feet high and was a good
seven or eight feet thick. It provided a screen between our front
stairs and the neighbors' fence. I had retreated there to be by myself, and when he appeared, I sat in a lawn chair with my hands
over my face. "Here, here," he said, placing his palm on my
head, "why the tears?"

I hadn't wanted to be discovered. I didn't really know how
to explain how I felt, except that I felt as if everyone and everything I cared about was being taken away from me. Harry was
gone. Marcia, Bill, and my classmates were terrified that the
Japanese would imprison them when they took over Manila,
which had just been declared an *open city,* supposedly a guaran-
tee the defenseless city would be taken peacefully. But we had
no idea what would happen. My brothers and I had American
citizenship through our father's naturalization. We were under
Mom and Bert's custody. She was Spanish, and he was Swiss,
both neutral countries. Would we be snatched away from them?
Then there was the call I had just had from Marcia. She had
asked, "You'd come to prison with us, wouldn't you? Aren't you
American?"

"Yes," I answered, feeling guilty, "but my folks aren't. Heck, I don't even know what I am anymore—Swiss, Spanish, American! I'm all mixed up."

"Well, I sure hope you're with us, Doreen. It would be terrible without you."

Terrible, without me? Terrible without her! I didn't feel comfortable sharing any of this with Bert, so I wept while he patted my head. "Go ahead and cry if it helps," he said softly. "Then come up and we'll have some mango ice cream—your favorite."

That made me smile. Mango was his favorite ice cream, not mine.

During the next few days we readied the house for our absence and packed some clothing to take to the Swiss Club, where all the Swiss families were told to gather for safety when the Japanese came into Manila. Candida and Eluteria agreed to stay at the house until we returned. Grandma was at Uncle Pepe's, a few blocks away on San Andrés Street, and the rest of the family were scattered around the city. Aunt Blanca and Aunt Lolita waited in their homes, knowing they would eventually be picked up with their American husbands.

Manila waited under a pall of deadly uncertainty. Retreating Philippine/American forces left burning oil refineries, and they destroyed ammunition dumps that would serve the Japanese. Large military contingents—the First Philippine Division, the Forty-fifth Infantry, Regiment of Philippine Scouts; the 91st, 71st, 31st, 21st, 11th, and Twenty-sixth Cavalry—all of which had been featured in the news and praised for their fight against the Japanese on their overpowering drive to Manila, now withdrew to the Bataan Peninsula. They traveled through Manila, mostly from the north and south, in ceaseless rumbling lines—trucks, armored vehicles, and cars—transporting weary soldiers and weaponry to Bataan. As I watched them from my window at night, their blacked out headlights glimmering eerily in the dark, I felt a deep hopelessness.

The last telephone call we received before our service was cut off was from my father. He explained to Mom that he was leaving for Corregidor as a civilian Army employee. It later came to light that he was working for the underground. I'm glad I didn't know it then. When he said goodbye, I knew I would not be talking to him for a long time. I could not cry. My stomach was tied in a cold knot.

On the afternoon of December 31, we loaded our Oldsmobile with our bags, pillows and blankets and traveled through empty streets, which had been choked with traffic only hours before. As citizens had fled frantically with their possessions to places of safety, cars, trucks, horse-drawn carromatas, carretelas, and unwieldy carts pulled by carabaos clogged the streets, causing bedlam.

The Swiss Club was packed with men, women and children, all vying for space on the first and second floors, where we would spend the night. Mom and I settled for a tight space under a window that faced the street. We placed our bags, a couple of light blankets and pillows on the floor. Bert and the boys found space in the men's section in another part of the building. Radios blared the news that the Japanese would take over the city by morning. All were being warned to stay home—to keep off the streets, and to remain peaceful at all costs. Peaceful, I wondered, how else could we be—defenseless civilians who didn't know what to expect?

I was staring out the window at the deserted street when I heard a familiar voice. "Hi, Doreen. I hoped I'd find you here." It was Liselotte Miller, a Swiss classmate, whom I had always admired for her ability to get along with everyone, and who now seemed like a long-lost friend.

"Hi!" I said, perking up. "I'm glad you're here, too."

We stuck together for the rest of the afternoon and evening. Nancy, who was a few grades behind us, trailed along while we wandered aimlessly, until it was time to eat a dinner of rice and tough stew. After dinner, we sat on the stairs leading to the second floor and tried to keep the conversation light, but we couldn't help drifting back to what we feared might happen in the morning. "I'm scared out of my mind!" Nancy cried, her brown bangs flicking as she wagged her head. Her exaggeration amused us, and somewhat minimized our fears.

After a restless night, fighting the hard floor and moving away from the window to get away from drops of hot oil that drifted in from the oil refinery fires, Mom and I awoke to the rumble of trucks and rough, unfamiliar, shouts from the street. Peering cautiously out the window, we saw the street alive with a procession of hundreds of trucks packed with Japanese soldiers, followed by an equal number of bicycles, and as many foot soldiers. Commands exploded around the invaders, who stalled every few feet, and then jerked forward. Wave after wave, they pushed by—trucks, tanks, bicycles, soldiers on foot, claiming Manila without having fired a single shot!

Overwhelmed by the overpowering display of military force below us, I could hardly breathe. The soldiers seemed to be all of one size, scarcely taller than I, and solidly built. Their uniforms were a light khaki, their pants, baggy; and their boots, dusty and heavily laced. They wore beaked caps with sun-flaps over their ears. There were guns everywhere, and some of the soldiers, officers, I assumed, had long swords hanging from their sides. But the worst thing about them was their angry shouting. Their voices were fiercely guttural. What were they saying? How would they treat us?

It wasn't long before we found out. A few hours later, several officers banged on the door and were met by some of the older men in our group. Stern-faced, waving his sword, one of the officers spoke in broken English. "Papers. See papers. All—line up!"

We formed lines from where we stood and dug for our papers. Bert and Mom sandwiched my brothers and me between them. After much pushing, shoving and yelling, an officer eventually reached us. He ordered Bert to empty his pockets onto a nearby table. I was repelled by his sweat-stained uniform. He smelled of grease and perspiration. After rifling through keys and loose change, he leveled a stony look at Bert and blurted, "Your children?" and pointed a stubby finger at us.

The color had drained from Bert's face; the muscles of his jaw were taut. I saw a familiar squint that indicated he was furious. Mom's chin rested on her chest. She did not look up. "Yes," he snapped. "Our children—fourteen-and-half; thirteen, and twelve." He handed him his passport first, and then showed him my mother's.

"Okay, okay," the officer hissed, "you go home. Keep papers ready."

I don't remember gathering our things and rushing to the car. Next thing I knew, we were riding down Taft Avenue, Japanese soldiers still swarming in the streets after their initial march into the city. Bert kept his eyes fixed on the road afraid that we would be stopped along the way. None of us spoke until we were several blocks from our house. It was then we saw a crowd of Japanese civilians cheering at some soldiers going by in trucks. They were waving Japanese flags and yelling, "*Banzai, Banzai!*"

My brothers and I ducked down on the floor of the back seat. The cheering blasted us as we slowed down to ride past them. Several faces grinned down nightmarishly through the glass. Hard raps hit the sides of the car. Just as Bert turned into our driveway, Candida and Eluteria, who had been waiting, instantly opened the gates. We piled out of the car, dragging our bags, and ran to the safety of the house. My breath was as shallow as if I had run a mile. Sheba yipped loudly and jumped up at us, followed by Maxie, a young fox terrier we had bought earlier as a companion for her. Sliding our windows shut to keep out the noise, we collapsed onto the living room furniture. One thing was certain—we were captives under the relentless control of a fearsome, unwelcome host—the Japanese Imperial Army.

VII

Whenever I revisit the memory of the Japanese occupation, it's as if I re-enter a windowless room and hear an only door slam shut behind me.

Fragments of memory come into clear focus. I remember Sheba jumped on my lap when we sat together to decide what to do. She was not particularly affectionate and it startled me to suddenly feel her small, shivering form nestle against me for comfort. I stroked her head and back, murmuring, "It's O.K. Sheba, it's O.K." Still, she kept shivering and looking up at me, her black button eyes fixed.

In the few moments of silence before Bert spoke, a sickening reality settled in around us. This was no nightmare. This was no dream. This was happening. Nothing would ever be the same. The question was as blatant as the cheering in the street: What should we do?

Bert rubbed the stubble on his chin. I had never seen his eyes looking so strained, yet when he finally spoke, his voice was strong and bore an edge to it. "We'll sit tight for a few days. Wait to see what these bastards are going to do. We'll set enough food and essential supplies aside for several days, so that no one will have to leave the house. After that we'll buy only what we need, and concentrate on not wasting anything. It's clear the Japs aren't here to help anyone, especially anyone who is white."

Mom, who had been sitting next to him on the couch, cleared her throat several times—always a sign she was nervous—but she managed to speak with authority. "Candida and I have a list of all the food we have on hand. We'll have to ration it. Two sacks of rice and mongo beans will keep us going for several weeks. After that . . ."

"After that, we starve?" Jim's fixed stare reflected his anxiety.

"No, no," Mom forced a smile, "we won't starve, but we can't waste what we have."

Bert's voice lost some urgency when he added. "Look, there's no need to panic. As soon as I can go out, I'll buy what we need. I plan to get some seed. We'll plant a vegetable garden. Buy some chickens. We'll manage."

"We'll manage," Mom echoed, "and work together. Do a lot things we haven't done before."

"Like what?" I asked, encouraged by the solutions taking form.

"Like helping out with all chores." Then she addressed Candida and Eluteria. "We'll help you with your work, and pay your salaries at what you're earning now, for as long as we can. Everything depends on what Bert can earn."

Candida and Eluteria both nodded. As anxious as we, they could see they would have security as long as we all joined together in a common effort. That included helping Fortunata, our lavandera, who had gone to stay with relatives during the emergency.

The cheering across the street had stopped. It was growing dark. We ate a light supper and went to bed, our bodies stiff from having lain on the hard floor of the Swiss Club, our minds overloaded, our ears ringing with words that exploded like headlines—*Japanese Occupation. Stay home. Remain quiet. Don't waste.*

We were glued to the radio during the next few days trying to find out what was going on. I was startled to hear that all American, British, Dutch, and other citizens of Allied nations were being picked up and taken to Santo Tomás University, which the Japanese had turned into a concentration camp. They were being rounded up, wearing the clothes on their backs, and being allowed to pack only one bag of personal belongings. There was no way to find out what was happening to them except through the grapevine. Our phones were disconnected, and until Bert was able to ride his bicycle to Uncle Pepe's, we would not know whether Aunt Blanca, Aunt Lolita and their families had been interned.

A wave of nausea rode over me when I thought about Marcia. Never in the past three years had we not been able to share our thoughts and feelings. Our lifeline was broken. I did not know whether I would ever see her again. There was no one else with whom I could share myself as I could with her. I had only my thoughts to turn to. It wasn't long before I began an inner dialogue with myself, and not long after, that I decided to start a diary. I wrote my first entry on January 7, six days after the Japanese occupied Manila.

I am sitting on my bed writing and trying to figure out where I will hide it so if the J's come to search, as they have started to do all over the city, they will not find my diary. Anything said against them is punished by beatings, imprisonment or death. Candida ventured to the Libertad Market, a couple of miles away by carretela, and saw several Filipinos, who had stolen some food from one of the warehouses, being beaten with ropes until they were unconscious.

Bert went to the office on his bicycle. He said the streets downtown are filled with military vehicles and a few carretelas and carromatas with riders who looked scared to death. Thank God, he wasn't stopped. It seems everything has become a crime, especially the crime *of failing to bow to the sentries. Word from the office is that business will resume in a few days, but only on a part-time basis, until it becomes clear what the J's plan to do about local businesses.*

The worst news is that all personal cars will be confiscated by the military. They claim all vehicles are needed on the fighting fronts, especially in Bataan. Heavy fighting is taking place there between our Fil-American forces and the Japs, who outnumber us—some say by five to one—and are far better equipped. How can we hold out? Bert says that rumors all over the City buzz with the hope that reinforcements will come soon.

I won't mention Marcia because it makes me cry. I can't imagine her in a concentration camp! And Bill is there, plus all the other kids from school. And Harry? I think about him constantly, and in my mind I see his bright face and hear his resonant voice as clearly as if he was standing here. I can only pray all of those I love who have vanished from my life are safe.

Bert stopped at Uncle Pepe's, where Grandma, Aunt Annie and Johnny are living. He heard Aunt Blanca and Aunt Lolita and their families were picked up three days ago and forced into an army truck. Aunt Blanca's house girl, who now works for Uncle Pepe, said it was terrible to see them squeezed in with many others at gunpoint and hauled away like so much cattle. There is no news of Dad, except someone told Uncle Pepe he was seen in Santo Tomás. That means he must have turned himself in as a civilian. Thank goodness. It would be terrible if he had been captured as a POW.

That's it for now. I must go to the kitchen to help prepare lunch. I am helping to run the household in ways I'm not used to. What an easy life I had! I must admit I do like to cook. Yesterday I made a beautiful fluffy pot of rice. I almost ran to the phone to call Marcia before I remembered the lines are dead and Marcia is gone.

I never would have believed our lives could have changed overnight as drastically as they did. The occupation army not only brought its tanks, guns, and planes into Manila, it brought a foreign culture as well. Within hours new rules and curfews were imposed, some of them strange and offensive, such as having to bow to every sentry that stood guarding military outposts, which sprang up everywhere. It was not enough to nod one's head when walking by one of these statue-like guards, one had to bow from the waist. For them it was a mandatory courtesy, for us, a humiliation, followed by a beating if we did not comply.

Manila shrank before our eyes. "The Pearl of the Orient," her outgoing, colorful spirit was suddenly inhibited by the presence of an obsessive military dictatorship bent on transforming her into an armed camp, imposing upon her free spirit the might of the Japanese Empire, with its goal to turn her, as well as all of Asia, into a "Co-Prosperity Sphere" for Asians.

By mid-January all car owners were forced to turn in their vehicles. The look of burning anger on Bert's face remains imprinted in my mind, as he stood by our car, ready to drive it to a location where the military were registering thousands of impounded cars from throughout Luzon. For him it was the ultimate effrontery. I believe that on that day something deep inside him soured. From then on it seemed he was less tolerant and quicker to anger against the Japanese. The lighter side of his character, which we had so enjoyed, dimmed.

A few days after we gave up our car, my brothers and I were summoned, as U.S citizens, to register at Santo Tomás. That morning a cold shiver in my stomach stopped me from eating much breakfast. As we climbed into a carretela an hour later, the shiver grew into a tremor. I tried to keep my hands from shaking as I held my papers. What would happen when we faced the Japanese at the camp? Would they imprison us? Would they let us go?

I had seen the historic old university before, but would not have imagined how its classical face had been altered. Surrounding the massive grounds around the ornate, gray stone buildings, tall barbed wire fencing had been erected, and at every corner stood a grim-faced guard. At the ponderous gate, also reinforced with barbed wire, two armed soldiers waited. Puppet-like we filed in front of them and bowed. I held on to Mom's hand so tightly I must have hurt her, but she only looked ahead, her face like chalk, set in fear. I did not dare look at Bert, for I knew rage must have been written all over his face.

One of the guards shouted and the gate opened. We were marched up the long walk lined with tropical trees, including fire trees, which on that day bore no red blossoms. My head swiveled right and left as I tried to recognize internees, their eyes apprehensive as we walked by. Some of them gave us a nod, and others, a cautious wave.

When we arrived at the Camp Commander's office, we were met by an American interpreter whom Bert recognized. I was still shaking so badly I was hardly aware of their greeting. The next thing we knew we were filling out papers. The interpreter explained our situation to the Japanese commander, who sat and looked at us through half-closed eyes, his jaw immobile, his mouth curved downward. For me, it was a face of disgust. He wanted to do as little as he could for us.

When it became clear that we were minors under the custody of our mother and stepfather, he barked out a sentence or two and we were given passes that supposedly assured our safety as American minors, released in the custody of neutral guardians. In addition, we were to wear red armbands whenever we were away from home, which would signal the Japanese to stop us and demand our papers. Feeling like branded steers, we hurried out as fast as we could. Sobs pushed their way up my throat. I held my breath to suppress them, feeling I would never take another breath. Just before we reached the gate, I spotted Joy, an Australian classmate whom I remembered as being very quiet and reserved. I had never come to know her, but as I passed, she recognized me. The sun glinted in her eyes and revealed her tears. I waved my hand at my side, and I knew that she would tell everyone she knew that she had seen me. Oh God, I thought, I hope she'll tell Marcia so she'll know we're O.K. The red armband would tell the rest.

By February my culinary skills had improved. I could now prepare an entire meal. I was complimented for my spaghetti sauce and for beef and chicken stew served with rice. I made the spaghetti sauce with fresh tomatoes still available in the market. Our own tomatoes would ripen in a few weeks. I chopped up six or seven tomatoes and sautéed them with onions and garlic before I added the chopped meat, which I had first put through our big metal chopper. We were still able to buy beef, although it was getting harder to find and its price had gone up so much that we decided we would soon be buying carabao meat, which was cheaper but much tougher. I disliked its grainy, musty flavor. It was a good thing it lost some of its characteristic flavor by the process of long, slow cooking, and by the addition of soy sauce to its gravy.

I'm not sure Candida was thrilled with my presence in her kitchen. I couldn't tell by her expression, which was always serious as she went about her business. She was a good teacher, very explicit in her instructions, making sure I understood, step by step. I had more fun with Eluteria who teased me by hiding stirring spoons and other kitchen tools so I had to ask her where to find them. Her eyes danced with mischief when she gave me false clues, until her aunt would lose patience and scold her. We'd laugh and use sign language to keep up the game behind Candida's back.

I was willing to learn to cook almost any dish except *lapu-lapu*, a long brown grouper with ferocious whiskers, which even hours after it was caught simply would not die. Candida would lay it out on the sink, still wiggling from the market, and strike it on the head with a mallet, while it flayed about. Even after she had decapitated the fish, its body would continue to flop, and finally lay still only when it was sizzling in the frying pan.

One afternoon, late in February, I was helping with dinner when a lapu-lapu literally flew off the counter and landed in front of me. "Catch him! Catch him!" Candida yelled as she, Eluteria and I danced around the slithering fish. Its slippery body was so distasteful to me I could hardly touch it. Remarkably, it was I who finally picked it up after it had lodged between my bare feet. "Ugh!" I hollered, while Eluteria doubled over laughing, and Candida's eyes shone bright with amusement.

When I turned to throw the prehistoric-looking creature into the sink, I saw my brothers smirking in the doorway. "Good job, Queenie!" Don cried, while Jim only chuckled and walked away.

Each day we worked in the house and vegetable garden. It was a magnificent garden, meticulously dug and cultivated in a square piece of land by the south side of the house. Bert and the boys did most of the digging, removing stubborn carabao grass, a variety of Bermuda grass with long, tenacious roots. By the time we laid out a dozen or so furrows the soil had been cultivated and felt so light it crumbled in our hands—perfect for tomato, carrot, bean, talinum (a kind of spinach), okra, and onion seedlings. When the young plants first sprouted, we made paper hats from old newspapers to protect them from the tropical sun. Morning and afternoon I carried pails of water from which I dipped a can and gently dribbled water into the small wells we kept cultivated around each seedling. The tender plants seemed to grow as we tended them, and it wasn't long before we were eating some of the vegetables. Having shared in the cultivation and growth of the garden, we all felt a sense of pride.

The chickens we bought—six white Leghorns and six Rhode Island Reds—were laying eggs in a few weeks. Even the pet ducks, Donalda and Wobbles, gave us eggs, although we used duck eggs mostly in sauces and other cooking. Duck eggs, like carabao meat, have a strong, gamy flavor.

We only left the house when we had to. Mom didn't want the soldiers to stop my brothers and me in the streets. They were unpredictable. Everyday it seemed Candida came back from the market with tales of horrible beatings she witnessed in the streets or she heard about in the rumor mill.

Rumors became one of our main sources of news. The local radio and newspapers were filled with propaganda. Rumors, on the other hand, always raised our spirits, for they could be counted on to temporarily keep up our hopes, whether they were true or false. This was especially true when they dealt with Bataan, where our Fil-American troops were battling over a quarter million well-equipped Japanese. General Wainwright was said to be holding a line midway down the peninsula. The embattled troops had eaten all of the 26ᵗʰ Cavalry's horses, but had repeatedly driven the Japs northward. General Homma was said to be losing face.

Rumors were ultimately verified or discounted by the Voice of Freedom, an underground radio station broadcasting from Corregidor's fortress. At our peril, we listened to the station every night. If discovered, we would likely have been thrown into Fort Santiago. The three-hundred-year-old fort prison, built during Spanish rule, was filled with citizens who had violated Japanese military laws. The dreaded Kempeitai, Japanese military police, ran the dungeon. Prisoners were chained in windowless cubicles, where Manila Bay waters would seep in at high tide, flooding the cells. Beatings administered with ropes and hoses resulted in crippling and death. Bert knew we took a big chance when we listened to Juan de la Cruz on the Voice of Freedom, but it was the one liberty we had left—to learn the truth about what was going on—a way to still feel attached to our Army and Navy and their heroic efforts.

It was at this dark time that the belief in an American counterattack and ultimate liberation began to grow like a small but urgent fire in our minds—a hope shared by a majority of the population: General MacArthur wouldn't let us down. The U.S. was too powerful to be defeated. Someday, maybe tomorrow or the next day, the tide would turn. It became for us a holy hope, without which our lives would have become increasingly threatened, increasingly meaningless—a pit from which there was no escape.

I thought of my family, Marcia, my classmates, and Harry within the framework of this hope. Come the liberation, we would all be together again. And we would do everything to survive to greet that day.

The ride by carretela to Uncle Pepe's on San Andrés Street was about two miles.

To get to his house we had to pass the Rizal Stadium, now a Japanese outpost. One morning in March, Mom and I decided to take a ride to visit the family. Bert wasn't in favor of our going. "Damn Japs are still stopping and searching people. There's no telling where they might be waiting. Why don't you wait a couple of weeks?"

Mom was as restless as I. It would be nice to change our routine and get out of the house for a couple of hours. We dressed alike in white blouses and flowered cotton dirndl skirts. We slipped on our wooden bakias. It was important to save our leather shoes because all leather goods were disappearing from the stores, and merchandise that remained was being sold at black market prices, three and four times overpriced.

Standing just outside our gate, we hailed a carretela and climbed onto the stiff wooden carriage, sharing the benches with two Filipino couples who got off about a block before we reached the Rizal Stadium. As we approached the fenced area, behind which the concrete walls of the stadium rose, I noticed six or seven soldiers sitting on the sidewalk on metal folding chairs. A group of Filipinos loitered across the street, their eyes fixed on the stadium gate. I leaned over and whispered, "Mom, look, soldiers!"

She grabbed my hand, "I know. We'll just go by them. They aren't sentries."

The cochero had just passed the soldiers when three of them jumped up from their chairs and came roaring at us. They pulled the reins to a stop, jolting Mom and me so we had to grab on to the wooden posts to keep from flying out of the carriage. The soldiers reached for us and pulled us off the carretela, shouting unintelligible phrases. One of them shoved me, knocking the breath out of me. My knees were shaking so badly as we were pushed in front of the group I felt I would lose my balance any second and fall. Mom held on to my hand. Her face had bleached to a dead white and her shoulders shook uncontrollably. One of the soldiers, a short, husky man with a complexion the color of copper, shoved his livid face inches from Mom's. At the same time another one poked at my armband.

At the moment when I was sure they would strike us down, two Filipinos raced across the street and cried, "Bow to the guards. Bow to them or they will beat you!"

Like two mechanized dolls, Mom and I began to bend from the waist—up-down; up-down! The soldiers took a few steps back and stared at us, their eyes steely with contempt as we agonized in front of them. Without warning, the husky soldier stepped forward again and spat at Mom's feet. The glob of spittle landed on one of her bakias and dribbled onto her bare toes. He squinted his bloodshot eyes at her, stuck out his jaw, and grunted his contempt. Another soldier came up behind him, yelled out a command and waved us away.

We raced for the carretela. The cochero had waited for us a half-block away and quickly helped us onto the carriage. As soon as we had climbed on, he kept repeating, "I'm sorry. I'm so sorry. I did not know. Early this morning when I passed, they were not there. There is no sentry. No sign. I'm so sorry."

It was weeks before we ventured from the house again, and then only after Bert checked out the nearby streets, although we knew they could post so-called guards anywhere they wished and at any time.

We were not the only ones who were abused at the Stadium. At the market Candida heard that the warehouse at the Stadium had been robbed by Filipinos looking for cigarettes. In retaliation the guards roughed up civilians who went by the Stadium, punishing them for what the looters had stolen.

A young Filipino who stole something from the American School outpost was caught and beaten on the sidewalk with wet ropes until his head swelled to twice its size, transforming his face into a grotesque mask for passersby to see. We could hear his screams for mercy from our house. I retreated to my room, closed the door and put a pillow over my head. My brothers watched the torture from behind the bars of our fence, and then reported what they had seen after the victim's screams faded into moans and were finally silenced by death.

I felt as if an enormous weight rested on my chest. I buried my sobs into my pillow that night, but found no relief. Although I had not seen the man's face, my imagination, triggered by his cries, painted so vivid an image, that it was as if I shared every blow. I would never again experience torture, real or imagined, and not cringe. It was as if death itself claimed me. There was no defense with which to fight this feeling of utter helplessness. I fell asleep hours later, having said my rosary twice and directing my prayers to a God, who seemed to have turned a deaf ear.

After the incidents at the Stadium and the American School outpost, I was more and more housebound. Routines kept me busy for a good part of the day. When I had time to myself, I wrote in my diary, reread favorite books, and played with Wobbles and Donalda. I became more reflective, more analytical. I found myself looking at the world around me with new eyes. I had a need to keep track of everything around me.

One morning while strolling around the yard, I stopped to take a good look at a male papaya tree that grew near a stand of banana suckers we had just planted. I had always admired its exotic grace. Short and tall, in various stages of growth, the tree's light gray-green trunk resembled a reptile's skin. As I stood under its large umbrella-like leaves which looked like open palms, I touched the decorative bark, pressing my fingers into the diamond-shaped scars left by branches discarded during its growth. The pattern of diamond indentations running up and down the trunk fascinated me, as did the star-like clusters of cream-colored flowers that hung from long tendrils, heady with perfumed nectar for tiny birds and insects destined to pollinate nearby female trees. The tree became an art object—a topiary that looked as if it should be potted separately in a patio. As I moved away from its protective umbrella of leaves, I reflected on how the papaya withstood harsh winds during monsoon season, bending and lifting against battering gusts.

As much as I admired the papaya tree, male and female alike, I did not like its smooth, melon-colored fruit with its thousands of dark gelatinous seeds. Plenty of sugar and lemon barely disguised a flavor that reminded me of vomit. What a paradox!

Everyone else in the family loved the fruit. Mom, whose nervous stomach worsened as the days of occupation lengthened into months, ate large slices of papaya daily to ease excessive acid brought on by nerves. She worried about our health, our safety, food, money—everything dealing with our well-being. In addition, she worried about the future and its dark unknown, which seemed to wait like a hidden snake ready to strike when least expected. It was that fear that gripped us all that made us try to hedge by controlling our lives as much as we could. We double-locked our gate and secured all doors to the house. We grew our own vegetables, raised chickens and ducks for eggs, and we saved things we would have normally thrown away— pieces of string, paper, rubber bands, rags, cans, bottles . . . When we weren't saving these items, we were fashioning them into things we needed: rags became patches; cans and bottles stored food and were used as containers, handy for whatever need arose. We used string to knit and crochet washcloths, socks, and even underpants, as these items slowly wore out. Pencils were worn to inch-long stubs; two half-used bottles of ink were rationed. We made paste from rice flour. There was little we did not save.

As we relied on our inventiveness, we also began to rely more and more on one another. Seldom was a decision made without family approval. As a result we grew closer together. My mother and I had never been openly demonstrative except to pat each other's arms affectionately or to hold hands when we faced fear, as we had at the Stadium. And it was after that experience, I found I sought her company more, especially when she lay on the couch in the late afternoon fighting an acid stomach. I sat on the floor beside her and we talked quietly. I often asked her if she thought Harry might still be alive in Bataan, which was, battle after battle, falling into the enemy's hands. Her voice low and drowsy, she would never tell me she thought he had survived, only that I shouldn't lose hope.

I knew she was open to my feelings, and I realize now, she shared a need to be close. She would pull my head down beside her shoulder and stroke my hair, sometimes so lightly I could scarcely feel her touch. Looking back, I sensed the bond between us grew into a spiritual chain, binding us together. I couldn't name it then, but now know it was a shared spiritual love that has stayed with me all my life—like a chain spun of an inner light.

On April 9 I removed my diary from its hiding place behind a loose tile on the bathroom wall and wrote:

This has to be one of the saddest days of my life. We heard the news on the radio: General King has surrendered our troops in Bataan. The city is alive with the news, added to which rumors that hundreds of our men got across to Corregidor, where they continue to fight. The Voice of Freedom still talks about reinforcements, but we are less and less hopeful. Bert says it's only a matter of time before we are totally defeated. That means Harry, if he is still alive, is a POW. I can't grasp the reality of it. The Japs are so cruel, their torture so horrible.

Last night before the news broke, a strong earthquake shook Manila. Our windows rattled and slid back and forth on their runners. Dishes flew off the shelves and crashed to the floor. We jumped out of bed and met in the sala. Don, Jim and I sat on the bare floor and felt it move beneath us, swaying us back and forth. It was an eerie feeling, as if we might fall through the flooring. The earthquake felt like a portent to the fall of Bataan, now an extinguished hope.

After lying in bed for hours listening to the crickets and the occasional shout from the street, I got up to write some more. What came to me is my first really serious poem.

A Message

Through the darkness of the room,
I could feel the warm night air.
Toward a dusky sky above,
I could see the bamboo loom
To a message whispered there.
In a forgotten prison camp,
I thought of him alone.
Across the depth of distance,
Came his message not unknown.
A star above fell softly into space.
It sailed across the heavens,
Past the mass of bamboo lace.
Before the darkness swallowed it,
I whispered his dear name.
A sweetness filled my little room.
I fell back and slumber came.

In an act of premeditated cruelty, the Japanese made the men of Bataan, some 68,000 sick, starving prisoners of war, march sixty-five miles from the tip of the peninsula to San Fernando, Pampanga, where they were packed into airless rail cars for the final miles of their journey to Camp O'Donnell in Tarlac province. Thousands dropped dead along the way—of wounds, dysentery, malaria and exhaustion. Those who stopped to rest or to relieve themselves were beaten or shot by the guards, whose obsessive goal was to herd them forward like animals. The prisoners were given no food or water for two days, and later in the march, only dribbles of water and single handfuls of rice. The water came from stagnant carabao holes. Many received no water or rice at all.

The Bataan Death March would have no equal. Bert cursed when he heard about it. I tried to shut the grisly scenes from my mind. I did not want to imagine Harry trudging in a line from hell.

At night we continued to hear the guns blasting from Corregidor. Enemy bombs thundered down on the rocky fortress with relentless and brutal accuracy. General MacArthur had been secretly transported to Australia. His last words, "I shall return," left us with bittersweet hope. When Corregidor finally succumbed on May 6, we were left with no foreseeable hope of an American return, except at some future time when U.S. strength regrouped and grew to eventually defeat the Japanese, as our Navy was beginning to prove by winning the Battle of the Coral Sea on May 7 and 8.

On June 4-6, the Japanese Navy was again defeated in the Battle of Midway, which further halted Japan's eastward trust.

VIII

When my father was imprisoned in Santo Tomás with his third wife Lettye, he asked Santiago, who had been his cook for many years, to bring us their cocker spaniel Scampy, a big black curly-haired male about a year-and-a-half old. Scampy was full of fun and mischief. The boys played with him on the grass, rolling around, pretending to wrestle him to the ground, while the dog drooled all over them.

Just after my fifteenth birthday in June, a friend of Mom's told us she knew of a female cocker who needed a home. The dog's name was Dina. She was small, sleek and very shy. Mom promptly fell in love with her, much to Sheba's chagrin. Dina was a one-person dog. She attached herself to my mother and would have nothing to do with the rest of us She detested Scampy and his puppy ways, and when she came in heat she did everything to escape his unrestrained affection. Scampy did not give up until he finally got his way with Dina. Making sure no one saw me standing furtively behind my bedroom window, I watched him finally overcome her resistance and mount her.

I knew from my many questions to Candida about the "birds and the bees," but I had trouble associating the making of puppies with the bizarre, distasteful act taking place before me. It was obviously a conquest for him, and victimization for her. Despite my repugnance, I couldn't take my eyes off them, until I was suddenly distracted by laughter coming from the mango tree outside my window. Horrified, I peered into the thick branches and was shocked to discover Don and Jim hidden among the leaves, enjoying the show. They had a full view of me. Jim leered as evilly as I had ever seen him and pointed an accusing finger at me. Don's eyes were filled with derision while he busied his mouth on a ripe mango, its juice dripping on his chin and onto his hands.

I stuck up my nose at them and hurried away as quickly as I could. I knew they would never say anything about me to Mom because they knew it would implicate them. The secret felt uncomfortable. Lying in bed that night I pondered on how humans might commit the act of reproduction. Was it possible we behaved like animals? How could such an act amount to anything but torture? I decided love could not play a part in such a wrestling match. I vowed I would never have children under such circumstances.

Two months later Dina had a litter of six fluffy black pups, three males and three females. We set up a nursery on some rags in my room. I observed them for hours at a time as they grew from round little nurslings to roly-poly balls of curly fur that loved to be hugged and played with.

We knew it was impossible to keep all the puppies. We already had four dogs we fed mostly on table scraps and soup bones. When the time came to sell the pups, there was one female, actually the runt, we named *Skippy*, with whom we felt we could not part. Mom was easy to convince, but Bert had reservations. "What do you think we'll do when our food runs out—eat the dogs?"

"Of course not," I cried. "I'll share my last meal with her. She's so little. She doesn't eat much."

Bert's lips curved into a reluctant smile. "Not now, but she will, Fifi, and then what?"

"Then we'll figure it out, dear," Mom stepped in.

He finally agreed, without really wanting to.

Skippy became queen of the kennel. We found another home for Scampy. He had become one dog too many and we knew he would adjust well to new masters. Unlike Dina, he was tough and exuberant and would reattach himself easily.

I would love to have played with Skippy and forgotten about anything else, but I had chores, which included schoolwork. In July we hired Mary, a Filipino teacher, who came to tutor us several times a week. Bert was still making enough money to pay her. I studied English, history and math under her tutelage. She was an excellent instructor and would take no excuses when I lagged doing my homework. I especially enjoyed poetry and spent hours reading Matthew Arnold's *Sohrab and Rustum.* I wish I could say the same about math. I just didn't think in numbers. Bert often helped me with difficult calculations, especially those involved in word problems. It was so easy for him, and he often raised his hands impatiently, saying, "Think! Just think it through, step by step. Now let's figure it out again: If car *A* starts out at 10 miles per hour and takes three hours to arrive in New York City, how long will it take car *B* at 15 miles per hour?"

My mind balked. I really didn't care how long it took either car, only that I was displeasing Bert by not being smart enough to figure out the problem. I did better when Mary started me on Algebra. I only had to memorize the meaningless formulas, or so I thought. Years later, the Algebraic process is a blank in my mind.

I had the same kind of conflict with piano. The mechanics of sight-reading caused me great difficulty. Once I memorized a new piece, which I invariably found difficult to read, I was able to play it by rote, easily and with expression. It pleased the family to hear my interpretations of Mozart and Beethoven. God help me, however, if I lost my way in a measure once I got started. My hands remembered mechanically, by rote, only if I didn't stop midway. I wish I could have been a better student. Mom, who earned a few pesos a week by teaching Spanish to one or two private students, paid for my music lessons with Madame Brimo, who lived about twenty minutes away by carretela. Mom must have felt that my lessons were worthwhile and I appreciated her sacrifice.

Early one afternoon in August, Mom discovered Dina in the driveway, her sleek black body shaken by convulsions. Her eyes rolled upward, she was frothing at the mouth. There was nothing we could do to save her. She died within minutes. Mom wept over her still form, repeating over and over, "Pobrecita, probrecita!"

We stood around in shock. What had happened? How could we have seen Dina at breakfast curled up happily by Mom's feet, and now she was dead? It made no sense.

After we buried her by the bamboo clump later that afternoon, Bert gave us his opinion on what he suspected had happened. "I think she was poisoned. Dina was sneaky. The garbage man hated the way she crept up on him and nipped at his ankles. I had to yell at her the other day when she went after him again."

There was no evidence that she had been poisoned except for the symptoms she displayed when she died, but it was the only explanation that made sense. Mom could not talk about it, and her eyes welled with tears when I said, "You know, that makes sense. Poor Dina would go after any stranger. Remember when her old owner told us she had a habit of running away, living on whatever she could find in the fields? God only knows what she ate that could have poisoned her."

Skippy, who was more like her father than her mother, gradually took Dina's place, for all of us except Mom, whose eyes always reflected a trace of sadness whenever she petted her. She loved Skippy deeply, but not in the same protective way she had cared for Dina. It was as if she and Dina had filled a profound loneliness in each other.

By Christmas the occupation Army had eased some of its brutal restrictions. Angry, unpredictable soldiers no longer routinely stopped us. The city had slumped into a suffocating routine. Nothing much happened. Many stores shut their doors, and places of entertainment closed down as well. Only horse-drawn vehicles and bicycles trafficked the streets, joining dogged military vehicles. *Go-carts*, covered carts pulled by bicycles, which carried a couple of riders, became popular when private cars were confiscated.

The internees in Santo Tomás were allowed to accept food from the outside brought in by relatives, friends or faithful servants provided they still had money to pay for it. Many internees were released on sick passes. We had notes from Aunt Lolita telling us that she, Uncle Tommy, and Carol were O.K. Aunt Blanca was released with Dickie and Steffie and went to live with Uncle Pepe. They joined a houseful of ten. Thankfully, they were spread out on two floors—a good thing when they bickered and cut one another off, sometimes for the flimsiest reasons.

When Auntie Carmen brought her first baby home, everyone was thrilled. Nuria weighed around six pounds, as I recall, and I got to hold her at her baptism. At a few weeks' old, she looked like one of Raphael's angels—curly brown hair, chubby cheeks and soulful eyes. I visited her as often as I could and loved to sit and watch my aunt nurse her. "Does that hurt when she sucks on you so hard?" I asked. Aunt Carmen looked up serenely. "No, no, not now, only when she gets more teeth, then—Ay!"

It wasn't long after that I saw her wince. Still, the picture they made was one of unity and peace. A belief in maternal love grew within me and fortified my spirit as I observed the bond between them.

Christmas, 1942, brought peaceful tidings. We were grateful to be with one another, to have a home. We felt secure within, which for the time being, no one could take away from us. It was not important to have a tree or decorations. I brought out a nativity set given to me at my Confirmation three years earlier. The eight bisque figures were made in Belgium and looked perfect on the buffet surrounded by several candles and a number of homemade gifts. I knitted socks for Bert and the boys and painted a small clay pot for Mom. I made penuche with raw brown sugar and coconut milk for Candida and Eluteria.

Bert gave me a lined notebook that would serve as an addition to my diary. He sketched a drawing of our house on the front cover. His gift to my brothers was a penknife for each of them—knives he had saved from his boyhood. Mom gave me a sapphire pin Ronnie had given to her when they were married. The boys made ashtrays they fashioned out of tin cans for our parents; and a vase for me, which they painted a combination of red, Jim's favorite color, and blue, Don's favorite. I planned to fill the vase with flowers and place it on my nightstand, where I knelt every night and said my prayers to pictures of the Sacred Heart and the Virgin Mary.

Candida and Eluteria cooked some bibingka for us. And so it went—a gift exchange all around and much laughter on Christmas Eve. We lit our candles, turned out the lights and talked. I felt so elated I suggested we sing carols. Bert immediately scoffed at the idea. "You know I can't sing a note!"

Mom, Candida, Eluteria, my brothers, and I sang anyway. *Silent Night* sounded good, first in English, then in Spanish, followed by a verse in Tagalog. Bert sat and smirked, but we knew he enjoyed it.

I won't forget that first Christmas under Japanese rule. No matter what went on outside, we shared an inner life together in the sanctuary of our home. We could only hope that right would never be taken from us.

The New Year brought good news from the war fronts. U.S. and Australian forces took over Buna in New Guinea. In February, our troops secured Guadalcanal, further halting Japan's march southward.

There was also good news from the camp. I received letters from Marcia, with a round-robin letter from my classmates. I was also delighted to hear from Bill. In part, Marcia wrote: *Doreen, do you know we get a thrill out of hearing a telephone ring, seeing a real kitchen, any movie magazine, going to the fourth floor and looking out over the walls, and millions of other little things that mean so much to us.*

There are so many rules and regulations. School takes up most of the morning. Then I help Mother with lunch, rest, go over to the dining sheds to study. That's fun. All the kids are there. We sing, tell secrets, giggle, and make a lot of noise. We have dinner at 4:30 P.M. This meal we usually eat "on the line." Mother lets me eat there with the kids. After dinner there is a basketball or baseball game; then we take a shower (only cold water) and go outdoors. At this time, there is music, swell music that can be heard all over the campus. Sometimes there is dancing, otherwise we sit and talk or play bridge (indoors). We do this till 9 P.M., when it's roll call. Everyone has to go to their buildings—men in the gym and educational building, women with children under 12 in the annex. The rest are in the main building. That's where we are with all the other girls.

Remember one day in school you drew my picture? Well, I sent home for my schoolbooks and in one of them I found that picture. I was thrilled! I am keeping it.

Don't worry, Doreeny, if something happens and I can't write to you it doesn't mean I've forgotten you. Because, how could I? I haven't forgotten any of our "cuckoo" secrets or told a soul, have you? Well, God Bless you, Doreen, so that we can be the same in a while. Love and kisses, Marcia

Bill wrote that he missed me and included some cartoons depicting life in camp. Lydia, a classmate, and one of Marcia's good friends intrigued me with one of her comments. *Liselotte came in the line last Sunday and we all spoke to her. She told us you had grown very pretty and gotten very serious.*

Her words made me feel I must have changed without realizing it. It also pointed out how far apart we were. I no longer felt like one of them.

A few weeks later I was encouraged to learn that temporary visitor's passes were being granted by the new Japanese Commander whose administration was less harsh than the previous one's had been. When Bert agreed to try to get a visitor's pass for Marcia, I was thrilled. I couldn't stop thinking about the possibility of her visit and spent time rearranging my bedroom, by setting aside things I wanted to share with her. Mom and I planned what we would serve on the days she stayed with us.

Her visit was something special to look forward to, even though I knew it might be difficult to arrange.

Several weeks went by, and then one bright afternoon Marcia arrived by carretela accompanied by an American guardian from the camp, who warned her she must be ready to return to Santo Tomás at the specific time and date indicated on her pass.

I met Marcia at the gate and we screamed with joy as we ran into each other's arms. It was Marcia—exactly as I remembered her—same smile, hesitant at her lips, but crinkling her eyes, eyes that said she had something secret to share; same honey-colored hair, and even the same green and white shirt and white shorts she had often worn, looking considerably faded.

The rest of the family greeted her with more hugs, after which she settled into my room. We had made up a cot for her, alongside which I placed a side table covered with an embroidered doily and decorated with a vase filled with red bougainvillea blooms. On her pillow I had splashed the last drops from a bottle of Midnight in Paris cologne.

Absence only seemed to have added depth to our friendship. We took up our conversation as if we had parted only yesterday. Mom called us two hours after Marcia's arrival to interrupt a two-hour, non-stop dialogue. It was time for dinner—a dinner that would have no parallel in the recent past. We had killed and roasted one of our hens, which we served with rice, gravy, carrots, and sautéed green beans from our garden. For dessert we had flan made with at least six eggs. Marcia was in awe. "I haven't eaten like this in years! How good it all tastes." She smiled as she helped herself to more chicken.

I could see the lights dancing in her blue eyes, and looking across at Mom, I caught the tender look she gave Marcia. "We're just so pleased you could visit. It means a lot to all of us."

The days went too quickly. Before Marcia left, we had one last talk. I told her how lonely I had been, how much I wished I could be with her and the kids. Her accounts of relationships in camp sounded romantic and exciting, and the group activities they shared, including dances, made me envious and sad not to be there. She countered by expressing envy at our still having a home and being able to eat so well compared to their meager rations of gruel made of rice and a few vegetables. They were still getting food from the outside through their cook David, but it was getting less and less available. "My Dad still has some money, Doreen, but we don't know how long the Japs will let us communicate with the outside. After that we'll starve." The corners of her mouth turned down and her eyes lowered.

"Oh, God, Marcia, don't talk like that!"

"It's true. There's never a day, ever, when we're having fun, when we aren't aware we're prisoners. They can come in anytime and kill us, you know."

I shuddered. "I don't know that we're much safer."

"You can hide. Maybe not successfully, but you're free to move around. We're not."

Tears brimmed in her eyes. I felt a lump grow in my throat. Words failed us. We put our arms around each other for a few moments before she had to gather her things to meet the carretela that was to return her to concentration camp.

I felt lost after Marcia left. I moped around the house until Don confronted me. "At least you had a friend come and stay. Be grateful, Queenie."

"What do you know about how it feels after a friend leaves?"

"All I know is you should appreciate having seen her and not mope about it."

He was right, but I wouldn't admit it. I changed the subject. "Things are so boring now."

He was willing to let it go. "Guess what? Mom and Bert are going out this afternoon."

I knew that meant we could have the run of the house. "Oh?"

"Yeah, we can put on a play."

I cheered up. Whenever our parents left for several hours we would invite Candida and Eluteria to join us in the sala, which was normally not allowed, while we performed impromptu songs, dances and skits. They sat comfortably on the couch and laughed with delight at our antics.

I usually directed our performances. When I was nine or ten, I loved to invent dances to music from the gramophone. Jim and Don kept the records wound up as I flitted about the room in a pink satin tutu. As a finale, the three of us marched around the room to Sousa's *Stars and Stripes Forever.* When I got older, I became too sophisticated for such antics. Instead I invented skits, for which we dressed up and made up comedy routines.

That afternoon Don dressed up in my turquoise, one-piece bathing suit. I tied a pink bandana around his head, and he did a flippant dance designed to place him in a position to catch an old, semi-deflated soccer ball Jim planned to throw from across the room. Don looked ridiculous in my bathing suit. It emphasized all the wrong bulges. The pink bandana and the smirk on his lipstick-smeared lips added to the effect. Candida and Eluteria clapped their hands to urge us on.

The skit ended unexpectedly when Jim heaved the ball to Don. Turning to do a pirouette, Don missed it! The saggy, old ball struck a tall blue and white, bas-relief porcelain water jug Mom had brought from Spain. It shattered into a thousand pieces. Candida and Eluteria sucked in their breath, and we three stood, stunned by the weight of our crime.

I forget what punishment we endured, but each of us knew it was deserved. Mom was crushed by the loss of one of her favorite possessions, and I have never forgotten how lovely the jug was. Handmade in Seville, I can still visualize it perfectly, with its intricate design of delicate figures gathered around various water wells.

We never told our parents that Candida and Eluteria were sitting in the living room with us when the accident occurred. The consequences would have been worse. That secret remained with us.

The entire question of domestic help became an enigma for me. When I was younger, I accepted the fact that Candida and Eluteria were part of our family, and yet weren't really related to us, more like friends who felt like relatives. Mom told me that was because we paid them, but that we would always treat them fairly and kindly while they worked for us. They were not social equals obviously, but as children we were with them all the time, and they felt like family. We played together in a way our parents could not. I recall sitting on the floor with Candida and having her show me how to use my toes to pick up objects from the floor. That led to a game where we would try to pinch each other's calves by using our big and second toes, working them like crab pinchers. Whoever got to pinch first—won. My toes became so prehensile I was even able to use them to open and close the faucets when I lay in the bathtub.

Candida also entertained us with stories. My favorite was the *Tale of the Little People*. She swore it was true: *One day my father went fishing off Batangas Bay. A storm blew up suddenly and his little banca was pushed way out into the Bay. It was swept up by angry waves. He thought he would drown when, without warning, he felt himself forced up onto a big, big black rock. The wind slashed at his face. He climbed up the slippery sides to an open place in the rock, which was like a basin. He looked down and saw hundreds of little torches. He could not believe what he saw. There lay in front of him a tiny, tiny village of little people, each one only three or four inches high. He was so surprised he could not move. He watched as they went about the village, which was protected from the storm by a piece of rock that hung over it like an umbrella.*

My father watched, and after awhile, he became sleepy. He slept for several hours. When he woke up, the village of the little people was dark. All the people were gone. The storm was over. He got up and returned to his banca, which was still lying on the side of the rock. He got home safely. Later, he tried to find the rock again, but he never could. He was sure he had not just dreamed about the little people. He really saw them.

"Come on, Candida, is that really true?" asked Don.

Candida's eyes, which always reminded me of the burnt sugar we used when we cooked flan, never wavered. "True. My father saw it."

"Aw," Don muttered. He wanted to believe the tale as much as Jim and I did. Consequently, we asked her to tell it again and again. Whether it was true or not, the story became part of our mythology, as much as it was Candida's.

My brothers spent several mornings a week walking to Libertad Market, where they bargained for corn to feed to our ducks, pigeons, and chickens. I don't know how they managed it, but they were able to return with full sacks, which they bought from the vendors at reduced prices. The sense of accomplishment and the feeling of independence that resulted from their negotiations led them to find ways to peddle their corn to people they met at the market who needed the grain to feed their animals. Soon they were into a small lucrative buying-and-selling operation. With the extra money, they bought things they needed or wanted, including tools and personal items.

Don became fascinated with the game of cock fighting. He decided to buy a rooster and train him to fight in a ring, which, if he won, could bring in several hundred pesos. His command of Tagalog was so good, he was able to talk a vendor into selling him a colorful young rooster he named *Napoleon*. Napoleon was gray and white. He sported the most beautiful red comb I had ever seen.

My brothers visited the cockfights to learn how to train a fighting cock. I watched them exercise the rooster, feed him special combinations of grain, and talk to him as if he understood what they were teaching him. What I did not expect was to see Napoleon lose his crowning glory for the sake of the gambling ring. Desperately, I tried to talk Don and Jim out of what they planned to do. To no avail. Don built a coal fire, which Jim tended until it guttered down to hot ashes. In the meantime, Don sharpened a knife with a pumice stone. It gleamed, thin and pointed, in the noonday sun. He demonstrated its sharpness by tossing a green leaf into the air and slicing it in half.

I hung around until I realized I could not stop the terrible deed. "You'd better go, Queenie," Don told me. "This is no place for you. Napoleon won't suffer. The second I slice off his comb, I'll cover the wound with hot ashes."

I stared at the captive rooster and turned on my heels. "You're criminals!" I yelled, running up the back steps, my hands over my ears to drown out whatever squawks the rooster might make.

When Napoleon stepped out into the ring about ten days later, he earned the cheers of several hundred Filipinos, who had bet their months' wages on the rooster, by slaying his opponent, a gold and rust male, as magnificent as he, with several swipes of the knife attached to his spurs. Heady with success, their pockets full of pesos, my brothers gloated over the win. In the following weeks, they won several more times. Then the inevitable occurred when Napoleon lost to an opponent slightly heavier than he and just fast enough to kill him first.

Napoleon's death put an end to cockfighting. Don continued to work in the chicken coop as diligently as he had before, but I never saw him befriend another rooster as he had Napoleon. I believe Jim, too, had been deeply affected by the loss of the rooster.

The piano demanded two hours of my time each day. I dared not waste either Madame Brimo's effort or Mom's investment in my musical talent, such as it was. I struggled with each new piece until I mastered it. Once I knew the notes, or I should say my hands knew it, I could never pick up midstream on the music. If I lost my place, I had to start again from the beginning. Madame Brimo despaired. She couldn't understand how I could ultimately play a piece so skillfully and with so much expression and fail so completely if I stopped playing in the middle of it. "You know it. It's right there in front of you if you forget." She would hold my delinquent fingers in her long pale hands and squeeze as if to infuse some sense into them.

I hated to leave her when the cost of each lesson was matched against the rising cost of food. "We just can't afford her," Mom told me one day. "Some of the money I'm making has to go for other things." Her expression told me she regretted it as much as I.

As it turned out, Madame Brimo had an advanced student who was giving lessons. Her name was Solita Cuervo. She played beautifully, and she welcomed me openly the first time I went to her home on Padre Faura Street in the Ermita district, not far from the academy where I had first started piano lessons. Solita was a vivacious brunette, as round and as expressive as Madame Brimo was fair, slim and tranquil. She was quick to detect my flaws and eager to show me how to overcome them. We laughed when I bungled difficult runs in Beethoven's *Pathétique Sonata* or Mozart's *Turkish March.* We took reasonable breaks and shared tall glasses of iced calamansi juice. Solita told me about herself, and I found I could open myself to her. I had been taking lessons for about two months when one day I told her about Harry. "I would give anything to find out if he's alive, Solita," I confided. "I think about him every day."

Her eyes went wide. Her mouth opened, then closed. She reached over and grabbed my hand. "Do you really want to find him?" she asked, her gaze intent.

My heart tripped. "Y-yes."

Her face drained of color. The red lipstick she wore contrasted against her pallor. "I can help you find him, but you must promise on your life you will keep it secret. The Japs would kill me, and you, too, if we are discovered."

My throat went dry. I couldn't speak. I stood up and placed my hand over my heart. "I swear, Solita, on my life!" I sputtered.

"Come," she said, "let's sit in the sala, where we can talk. I'll tell you what I know."

She led me to the living room and we sat down on a flowered settee. In barely audible whispers, she told me she was working with an underground group, headed by someone code-named *U,* who was able to smuggle notes and money in and out of Cabanatuan, the POW camp to which all the U.S. prisoners had been transferred from Camp O'Donnell. She explained how nuns and priests were allowed in with vegetable carts to deliver small rations of vegetables to the prisoners, mostly to the ones who were in the camp hospital, seriously ill with dysentery and malaria. The notes and money sent in by relatives, friends, and members of the underground were hidden among the produce in the carts. When the POWs responded, they slipped their notes to the clergy, who hid them in the carts and delivered them to the underground. Couriers like Solita took action from there. I was told to invent a code name for myself so that, if and when she found Harry, my name would not appear on the return address.

I felt as if my feet had grown wings when I ran for a carretela home. I couldn't wait to tell Mom and swear her to secrecy. When I did, her reaction was that I share the information with Bert and the boys. "We're all in this together," she said.

She was right. All five of us wrote letters to Harry. Mine was the longest. It covered a sheet and-a-half of lined notebook paper. We were careful not to say anything against the Japanese, concentrating instead on our everyday lives, the household routines, our vegetable garden, the dogs, and schoolwork. I mentioned how much we hoped he was all right and to please let us know if we could help him. Bert offered to send him a little money. In all, we wrote two-and-a-half pages. I followed Solita's instructions by folding the sheets of paper in half and then (longwise) into fourths, so that I ended up with a tube, which I folded tightly back into itself. This resulted in a folded note that was two inches square. On the outside I printed his name. It felt so good to write it down: *Harry Terrell, Cabanatuan.*

Weeks went by. Then one afternoon in August, Solita led me to the sala. She looked around the room, first peering out the windows. Quickly, her green flowered skirt rustling against her calves, she hurried across the room to a round wall mirror. Lifting it off its hook, she ran her fingers alongside the wooden panels behind it until she found a loose board. She mysteriously slid it back a few inches to reveal a secret opening no larger than the size of a small envelope, and only a couple of inches deep. She reached in and pulled out a note folded in the same way I had folded the letter to Harry.

She slid the panel back in place, re-hung the mirror, and stared triumphantly at me. I had a feeling similar to that I experienced riding on a fast elevator. My heart leaped. My breath caught. I didn't know whether to laugh or cry. Solita began to dance around, crying, "He's alive, Doreen. He's alive!"

I was finally able to open my fingers, which I had clenched around the note. Holding the tiny square of folded paper to the light, I saw my code name printed in pencil: *Alan Greene*, followed by *Via U % SS*. Once again, I experienced the elevator sensation and was about to open the note when Solita cried, "No, No! Wait until you get home. I know you'll cry."

And cry I did, but not until I arrived home after a nerve-wracking carretela ride, where I imagined every soldier on the streets would stop me. Once I arrived home, I ran into my room and shut the door, leaving Mom and the boys staring after me.

When I opened the note, I paused to study Harry's familiar penmanship. To this day I can recall exactly how he formed his letters. Tears spilled as I read:

Dear Doreen, I don't know of any way to start, except that I am about the happiest man on earth now. I have been counting the days until I could look you up and find out that you are all coming through all right. Doreen, I could not forget you, and I often prayed that our horrible host had not pulled any of their torture on any of you.

I have had many close experiences. Last year, I caught malaria and was expected to die, but I outwitted the old man with a scythe. Then I contracted dysentery and was moved to a place where a fellow had to be a pretty good man to come out walking. Now, I'm in as good condition as a person can be on a diet of rice three meals a day for the past twenty months. We work awful hard, long hours in the sun every day and sleep on rough bamboo slats at night. But no matter how tough they make it for me, I'm going to grit my teeth and pray that it will not be too long before I can once again think for myself and not have one of these little fellows standing over me with a club.

I have saved up an awful lot of things to tell you in these long months and I assure you I will be a very good correspondent. Keep your chin up, and I am always anxious to hear from you. Yours, Harry. P.S. Please excuse the paper and penmanship.

I pressed his letter against my breast and lay, face down, on my bed. I sobbed into my pillow until I heard Mom's knock. Opening the door, I fell into her arms, crying, "He's suffered so terribly, Mom!"

She held me until I was able to take a breath. "Here, read the letter. He's also got a greeting for you, Bert, and the boys."

We all sat down that night and responded to Harry. Bert slipped thirty pesos in with our letters. Then frowning, he lowered his voice. "We're into dangerous ground. There's no way I think we shouldn't write to Harry and help him, but we absolutely have to exercise every caution. We could end up in Fort Santiago. People have been tortured and killed for less. Fifi, you are in the most danger because of your connection with Solita. If she gets caught—God help you. God help us all."

My mother's face reflected his fear. A sharp line pinched between her brows. She pursed her lips and nervously cleared her throat. "We have to keep our connection with Harry an absolute secret. Tell no one. Then trust in God we'll be protected."

The horrifying specter of being caught by the Japanese Kempeitai never left my mind, but the thrill at having made contact with Harry overshadowed that fear, for the time being.

On September 18, we heard from Harry again. I could not wait until I got home to read his letter.

Dear Doreen, I hope I've not kept you waiting too long. I had a talk with a fellow about mail, and even if I do go on a new detail, we can correspond, as my mail will be forwarded to my new location. The only difference is that it may take a little longer time.

Now for a little history. When I first came to O'Donnell, the first camp I was in (we marched from Bataan), I started working in the kitchen. While many men were profiteering, I was helping

*out some fellows from my squadron and asked no returns. One
week after my coming there, I was doing several men's work in
the rain on top of a huge rice vat. I passed out. Next, we came to
Cabanatuan, where we had to sit out in the sun, and I came near
going out again. I tried to work here, but malaria had me and I
could not go on. The day before going to the hospital, I begged a
cup of carabao blood from a carabao that was being butchered.
I stuffed this down.*

*I was afraid of the hospital, and no one expected me to re-
turn. I finally received a little quinine from the Medical Corps
here (good people). Then I came down with dysentery and was
moved to a shack with my commanding officer, an awful place.
Almost every morning I would awake and try to awaken the guy
on the bamboo beside me. No use.*

*Next, the officers and the medics received a little pay, and
they were eating good food, but that did not help me. I started
catching rats to earn tobacco, which I traded to buy a few neces-
sities, salt and a few eggs. Thank goodness I do not smoke. Well,
I ran out of rats (what a business), and now I'm going out on the
farm, barefoot, from the break of day until dark.*

*I hope I've not bored you with this dull letter. Doreen, dear,
I must write fast, as I must collect my rags and get ready for a
very early take-off from here, Sunday, sooner than I expected.
I'll pray connections are not broken. If they are, I'll come to see
you the first chance I get. As ever yours, Harry*

When I finished reading, Solita looked at me and said, "My
God, Doreen. You look pale as death. What did he say?"

I clasped my hands together and shook my head. "He's been
so sick, Solita. And now they're moving him. I may never hear
from him again. Read it," I said, handing her the letter.

I could see Solita shared my fears after she read the letter. "I
don't know what to tell you, except that the underground has
been able to follow POWs from one camp to the other. Don't
lose hope."

I wanted to believe her but I had a feeling that it would not
be easy. Having just found him and established such a meaning-

ful connection, I had a sense of foreboding that, because he was being sent to another camp, all ties would be broken. After Mom, Bert and the boys read their notes from Harry, my spirits momentarily lifted. They were so happy to know the letters and money we sent had helped him. He wrote:

Hello Maria, Bert and the boys, I'm heading I don't know where, but the going will probably be tough. At least I'm not leaving the islands, and the tougher these fellows get, the more they will receive later.

I should give you a growl for trying to help me. You seem like my own parents, and your gift of letters and money has made life worth living again. KEEP 'EM FLYING, Harry

That night I slept with his letters under my pillow. Having read them several times, I went over his words again and again in my mind—a great comfort, as was the scent of the paper on which he wrote. It smelled of the sun, and held the mystery of his touch.

IX

News of Allied victories in the Solomon Islands was not good for the Japanese. They had clearly begun to fight a defensive war. Their retreating Army and Navy had to be maintained. Where were all the food and supplies coming from? The Philippine rice basket was available for them to plunder. More and more rice was confiscated from the tenant farms and from the markets. The rumor mill buzzed with tales of Japanese soldiers loading cargo ships full of rice, some of it reportedly going to Japan, where the war-deprived citizens were beginning to starve.

We felt the shortage in Manila. A ganta of rice (just under a quart of dry measure) was priced many times what it had been a year, or even six months earlier. Filipino tenant farmers in the provinces were being robbed of their harvests. Candida told us her father had written her that the Japanese had confiscated over half their crop. "Maybe I will have to go home to Batangas to help my family. Farming is very poor," she told Mom, lines of worry on her usually smooth, golden-brown complexion.

On November 15 a typhoon hit, bringing floods and more chaos to the islands. Rain, rain, rain; then the winds roared in, and whipped and blew apart all that was in their path—nipa shacks, tin rooftops, trees of every variety, and even some telephone poles. I recall watching the mango tree outside my window doing a crazed dance. Its limbs littered the ground. The rain hissed down in blinding sheets, transforming our peaceful green yard into a blowing, colorless-gray scene. All animal and insect life were hidden in mysterious places, and we, fairly secure in our house, waited for the eye of the typhoon and the ceasing of the whirlwind downpour.

The flood that followed the storm caused a second round of catastrophes. Over twenty inches of rain had fallen in twenty-four hours. Those who had lost their homes found they had no-where to go. Streets had turned into rivers, six to eight feet deep in many locations, including our yard. We watched the muddy waters rise and stop miraculously just as they reached our top step. Don called me from that step, on which he stood, keeping track of the rising waters. "Doreen, come quick, Donalda and Wobbles are in trouble. They have been in the water too long," he cried.

When I joined him, I was astonished to see our pet ducks barely moving in the murky water, their red crests paled to an anemic pink. Don pulled off his shirt. "Let's swim after them and bring them in the house with the chickens and turkeys."

He made sense. Obviously the ducks had had no place to roost and had exhausted themselves. We had rigged up the bath-room as a temporary coop for as many fowl as we could squeeze into the area, including two turkeys—a male and female, recent-ly purchased—named *Gulliver* and *Lilliput*.

Don was already swimming toward the ducks when I threw off my bakias and went in after him, fully dressed. "Wait!" I shouted, "I'm coming in!"

"Hurry!" he sputtered, spitting dirty water out of his mouth.

The flooding was so deep I couldn't touch bottom. It took us several minutes to catch Donalda and pass her on to Jim, who had heard us and waited on the top step to take the duck into the safety of the bathroom. Wobbles resisted by swimming away with all the strength she had left. When she got entangled in some bushes by the north fence, which separated us from our neighbors, we grabbed her. Don held on to her feet, while I held down her wings. It was a slow swim back across the yard. We held the duck between us and paddled with one hand, keeping ourselves afloat by kicking our legs. We went under several times and came up spewing water, barely avoiding swallowing the foul stuff.

Jim reached out both hands and grabbed Wobbles, by then so weak she offered no resistance. We shook some of the water off ourselves and entered the house, still dripping. I glanced back at the street just as the bloated body of a dead horse drifted past our gate.

"Come on, Queenie," Jim beckoned, "see what's in the bathroom." He grinned, the dimples deep in his cheeks.

The bathroom was a mess. The tile floor was covered with droppings from the chickens and turkeys. "What?" I questioned. "I don't see anything."

"Look again," he said. "Look inside the hat."

Sure enough, he had placed a white-brimmed straw hat under a roost made from a broom handle secured between two walls. Lilliput teetered on the long pole. Taking a closer look at the hat, I observed a turkey egg lying in its nest-like center. "Oh, my, gosh," I laughed. "What a dumb bird! Good thing you thought of the hat."

My brother beamed. The day before, Lilliput's egg had smashed on the tile floor when she dropped it from the roost.

The weeks before Christmas passed without news from Harry. He had obviously been transferred from Camp I, Group II, Building 30 in Cabanatuan and was in a location where he couldn't be reached by the underground couriers. There was bad news from Solita. She told me her line of communication had temporarily shut down because the Kempeitai had caught some of the couriers delivering messages. They had ended up in the dungeons of Fort Santiago.

I heard of a case that came too close to home. One afternoon in December, I went to visit Liselotte. When I didn't find her at home, I walked a few more blocks to see Carmen, whom I had met through Georgie, another friend, whose mother was close to mine, and who was out on a pass. Carmen met me at the door, looking anxious. "Come in. I have bad news," she said, shutting the door after me. Her dark mane of hair whipped against her round, pale face. She was a little shorter than I and more buxom. I admired her upbeat attitude. She had a habit of talking very fast, often in a mixture of Spanish and English, and she laughed easily. That afternoon she was as sober as I had ever seen her. "You know Miriam, don't you? She visits often."

I nodded.

"Well, Miriam's sister Betty has been involved in the underground, sending letters to Cabanatuan."

"Oh," I whispered, my hands clenching. I had not told Carmen about Harry.

Carmen shook her head. "It's terrible. The Japs picked her up, with some other people. Someone had ratted on them. They're in Santiago."

"No!" I barely breathed. Was Solita among them? Poor Betty, what had happened to her? "Is she dead?" I forced out the question.

"They nearly beat her to death. Kicked her in the kidneys. Kept her several days and then threw her out because they couldn't pin anything on her."

"Thank God," I said, a wave of fear passing over me, making me feel as if I had no legs to keep me up. "Who else?"

Carmen pressed her lips firmly together, "Not sure, three or four others. They'll die in that hell hole."

I couldn't wait to leave to check if Solita was all right. On the way home I stopped by her house. When she came to the door she looked at me, a half-puzzled smile on her face. "It's not your lesson today," she said, "but come in."

"I won't stay. I just wanted to know you're O.K."

Her smile faded. "You heard about the Japs rounding up some of the . . ." she didn't finish, casting a sideways look around, and then continued, ". . . some of the couriers. So far, I'm not involved."

I grabbed her hand. "Gracias a Dios!"

"Thanks be to God." Then she added, "Time to lie low."

Her words rang in my ears: *Time to lie low.* All the way home, the carretela jogging over ruts on Taft Avenue, chanted, *Time to lie low. Time to lie low.*

Hope of hearing from Harry, or about him, seemed lost. It was as if a dark sheet had lowered on my world, a world already darkened beyond anything I had ever dreamed. I didn't even look forward to Christmas. It came under rainy skies, unusual, in a time when the monsoon season was supposed to be over.

A single candle burned over my nativity set. Our homemade gift exchange was more modest than it had been the previous year, but we were together in the candlelight, and that was what mattered. I should say we were not quite all there. Eluteria had left for Batangas to help her family in the rice fields. We didn't know how long Candida would be with us. I studied her face in the flickering light, and felt a wave of affection. She caught my glance and smiled. Her perfect teeth gleamed, her eyes fixed on mine in special acknowledgment—a look I felt was just for me. I'll remember her always, just in the way she looked at me across the candlelight.

"Why so serious, Fifi?" Bert's hand on my shoulder startled me. "Don't you want to open my present?" he asked, placing a small package obviously wrapped in twice-used tissue paper.

"Sorry," I said, taking the gift from him. I opened it carefully. In my hands I held a small hand-blown glass clown waving a red balloon, an art object Mom and he had brought back from Venice. He knew I had always admired it. Unbidden tears stung my eyes. I tried to swallow the thickening in my throat. "I love it. Thanks so much," I said, so softly he had to lower his head to hear me. "Here's mine for you." I handed him a handkerchief I had stitched from a piece of worn sheet. In one corner I had embroidered *B* in navy blue thread.

I could tell he had read my reaction when he gave me the glass clown. He made sure he looked at me unwaveringly when he thanked me. "It's really very attractive and personal. You've done nice embroidery. Very nice. Thank you." I did not detect his usual teasing tone. His look was direct and sincere.

My mother's gift had no equal. It was a sapphire and diamond ring she was given by a close friend named Dora, the wife of a family friend we called Uncle Cecil, who befriended us in France while we lived there after Mom's divorce, and before we returned to the Philippines. Mom treasured the ring. Giving me something that meant so much to her stirred a deep reaction of love and gratitude in me. Speechless, I put the ring on the third finger of my right hand and held it to the light of the candle. It had always reminded me of a jeweled flower. Perfectly round, several tiny diamonds winked in a hammered platinum center, which was surrounded by a circle of miniature rectangular sapphires. When I looked up I could barely see my mother's face through my tears.

On January 6, 1944, Three Kings' Day, we joined the family at Uncle Pepe's to celebrate *El Día de Los Tres Reyes,* in the Spanish tradition. We exchanged no gifts but put together a simple merienda, a tea replete with bibingka, bread, papaya jam, tea, coffee and iced calamansi juice.

I wore a dirndl skirt Mom and I made from some curtains that hung in the dining room. The fabric was a cotton weave, featuring white flowers on a light green background. There was enough material to cover an old umbrella, which we turned into a colorful sun parasol. I had never had a matching skirt and umbrella, and I received compliments from the family.

We were quite a crowd—aunts, uncles, mothers, fathers, sisters, brothers and cousins, the youngest of which were Pepito, still in Carmen's arms, and Nuria, who chattered endlessly, her brown curls, a halo around her diminutive head. Cousins Johnny and Dickie expended their nine-year-old energy by shouting and racing all over the house. Stephanie followed them without ever catching up.

Missing were Aunt Lolita and Uncle Tito's families. It was too far for Uncle Tito and Aunt Rosemary to come from San Juan. In the din of the party, they were barely missed, but not forgotten.

The merienda offered an opportunity for non-stop talk. As the afternoon wore on, I got down on the floor and played soldiers with Johnny, Dickie and Steffie. Having tutored the boys for months, I related well to them. The good guys—Americans, of course—always won the war!

The adults pursued two subjects—the war and deteriorating conditions in Manila, in particular, the food shortages. We were all saving for the days ahead, a future heavy with imminent specters of starvation and battle. The allies were winning the war in Europe and the Pacific. None of us had forgotten MacArthur's promise—*I shall return.* But was it a false hope or a looming reality? I agreed with Uncle Pepe who said, "I feel it in my bones. There's going to be one hell of a battle for the Philippines, right here in Manila."

No one disagreed. There was only speculation as to where and when. I shuddered. Mentally, I could imagine Manila burning, and we, running helplessly for shelter. It was an image so vivid it haunted me, especially at night when I heard the rumble of military activity in the street and listened to soldiers yelling on the grounds of the American School.

Grandma came home with us after the merienda. Mom suggested she get away from the chaos at Uncle Pepe's for a few days. Aunt Blanca and Aunt Annie had been quarreling constantly, mostly over children's issues. They had come to blows. Grandma had tried to intervene by standing between them. My two aunts had been hitting each other furiously with a couple of high-heeled shoes! They were so distraught they ignored Grandma's pleas, and inadvertently struck her on the head. As Grandma crumpled to the floor, both women came to their senses, helped her up, and apologized. Still at war, my aunts continued to refuse to speak to each other. Their tension had been palpable at the merienda. I had avoided them. It made no sense for them to be so petty, but I had to excuse them because they lived crowded together and were stressed by the weight of the occupation. Still . . .

Bathed in a peaceful sunset, Grandma and I sat and watched the sun go down over the bamboo trees. We ignored clouds of steam rising from the showers in the low buildings on the other side of the stone wall, and concentrated on the haloes that bloomed around the bamboo's ethereal leaves, shimmering in green and gold. "Qué lindo," Grandma commented, captivated by the beauty and visible calm, the opposite of what she had put up with at Uncle Pepe's.

Echoes of my uncle's prediction about a battle in Manila lingered in my mind. Seeking assurance, I asked, "What do you think, Belana? Is Uncle Pepe right about a big battle in Manila?"

Looking away from the dimming light playing in the bamboo, she focused her deep, lucid eyes on me. "Precaución es vida," she said gravely.

Precaution is life I repeated. Did she agree with her son? I probed further. "So you think he's right?"

"Yes and no," she answered, getting up and folding the garden chair. "Only that we must be ready for it and take every precaution."

It bothered me that she was not willing to answer one way or the other. I suppose I wanted her to allay my growing fears of facing a fiery end to the occupation. "I'm afraid he's right. I imagine a terrible battle," I said. "In my mind I see fire, destruction and death. It's so terrible that I lie awake at night."

A glint of alarm sparked in her eyes. "No, querida, you'll drive yourself crazy by useless worry. No one knows but God what will happen. Trust in Him."

Trust in Him! Like *a non-swimmer on a rocking raft?* Trust in Him, because when you are trapped, in whom else can you trust? The thought weighed like lead. I tried once more to force her to be most specific. "So you think God will save us?"

"God promised only to save our souls, if we turn to Him. Our bodies are dust. We won't need them in Heaven."

She had evaded me once more! Save our souls? How could we be sure we had souls? The question begged an answer. I sighed heavily, folded my chair and followed her up the stairs, stopping to pick up a ball of string she had dropped, from which she was knitting a pair of red socks for Nuria. I knew one thing—Uncle Pepe was right. I felt it in my bones, too—the enormous weight of an impending battle, like a black and white scene in a movie, where distant enemies line up on opposite sides of a far-off horizon.

Because persistence was part of my personality, I approached Candida with my loaded question. I knew she could be trusted to speak her mind, good or bad. I caught her in the kitchen, her hands white with flour as she prepared fish for dinner. "Can I talk to you?" I asked, knowing she would not leave her task. I watched her hands turn the fish in the flour and heard their soft, *pat-pat-pat.*

She must have sensed I was about to trap her with another of my eternal questions. She did not look up. Barely nodding her head, her hands patting faster, she waited. "Tell me if you think there will be a big battle when the Americans come back," I pressed.

Unabashed, she continued coating the fish. "Of course," she answered. "Do you think Japón will give up the Philippines?"

"No," I countered. "I think they will fight, but the Americans can beat them, so the destruction maybe won't be too bad?"

She stuck out her jaw, reflected for a moment, and added, "*Bahala-na*—what will be, will be."

I knew that was the end of our conversation.

Not satisfied, I approached Don that night while we lay in rooms separated by a wall that stopped short about a foot before it reached the ceiling. We could talk back and forth as we used to in Protacio Street. Don and I could read each other's minds. When I asked his opinion about my conviction regarding a future battle, he said, "You sound like you want everything to be O.K. You want me to say, '*No, it's all going to end peacefully.*' You're really scared, aren't you?"

At first I couldn't answer. I concentrated for a moment on the shrill call of the crickets in the quiet night. Then I said, "I-I guess I am. I have a horrible vision of running from fire, bombs falling, screams . . ." I heard him clearing his throat. "Like a premonition?" he asked. The springs on his bed groaned as he shifted his weight.

"Yes. I can see it in my mind. It gives me the shakes."

"You may be right. The Japs aren't going to give up. You know how they are—maniacs. They follow the law of *Bushido.* It's their Samurai tradition—*Defeat the enemy at all cost. Give up your lives if necessary.* Yes, I agree. Because the Americans want the Philippines back, there will be a huge battle."

I finally had my answer. "Don?"

"Yeah."

"Do you think God will protect us?"

He didn't respond for a second or two, and then in a resigned tone, he answered, "I hope so."

"Me, too," I muttered, feeling the relief of sleep coming on. I actually had three answers: Trust in God. What will be—will be. Yes, there will be a battle—how big, no one knew.

I decided it was time to devote more time to prayer. True, I went to the La Salle Chapel on Sundays with Grandma, but a lot of my prayers were rote, often a frantic repetition of words, recited to ward off bad thoughts. I kept asking God's forgiveness, for *this* for *that,* but never directing my prayers to Him and truly expecting mercy. After all, the priests at confession knew I'd be back, confessing again and again, the same sins—lies, disrespect to parents, and the worst one, violating my body. You'd have thought they owned me—body and soul. I had to report how I had touched myself in the most personal places. Even my thoughts regarding the enjoyment of those dark, sinful activities had to be confessed. I was sure the priests were fed up with me. God, then, must surely be disgusted. It never occurred to me that every other teenager I knew must face the same dilemma, especially if they were Catholic.

I dared not mention any of this to my mother or to my friends, Liselotte, Carmen, Georgie or Miriam, whom I saw periodically. It was my secret, guarded by guilt; and the priests, Fathers Kelly and Monaghan, and of course, God's. Asking for His protection when I was violating his commandments was not only senseless, it was hopeless. There would be no relief. As fears of war circled closer, my anxieties could only grow.

One sultry afternoon in March, two Japanese soldiers clanged the chain on our gate, and, we assumed, demanded that we let them in. Neither spoke English. They exploded into a tirade, behaving as if we understood their demands. Bert was at the office, and the boys at Libertad market. Mom, Candida and I clung together after we opened the gate, as if doing so would send the message that we stood firmly together. I couldn't have said a word if I'd tried, but stayed braced like a mannequin between Mom and Candida.

The soldiers circled around us as if we were prey, their hands gesturing here and there. Except for a firm set of their jaws, their faces were without expression. After encircling us twice, one of them drew a deep breath through clenched teeth and hissed it back out again. Simultaneously, Mom took a step forward and swept her hand outward in a gesture that indicated they could go wherever they wished.

Their bodies rigid and their leather boots squeaking, they toured the garden, twice around the house, looking up and down and around the yard as if they were mentally measuring specific distances. We remained cemented in place. I gripped Mom's hand. "Shhh, don't move. They'll be gone soon," she whispered.

So as not to concentrate on the soldiers, I stared up at the sky and forced myself to watch a large white cloud scudding by, momentarily covering the sun so that the branches of the mango tree under which we stood cast a pool of shadows around us. Oh, God, protect us! I prayed silently.

Within a few minutes the soldiers marched around us once more, and then out the gate, kicking gravel up with their boots.

They left without a backward look. Gathering our wits, we were heading for the house when we heard, "Hey, Maria, come over a second." It was our neighbor, Joan Camon, an American, married to Faust, a Filipino she had met while in school in Detroit. She was out of camp on a pass that verified she was a Filipino citizen.

When we met her at our mutual fence, I saw her eyes were wide with excitement. "I'm so glad they didn't hurt you," she said, lowering her voice. "I thought you'd like to know what Faust heard. Seems the new Naval group of Japs in the school are looking at houses to occupy around here. They were here yesterday, and I think that's what they were doing at your place just now."

That night I wrote in my diary: *What's the use of planting vegetables and building a shelter when any day the Japs can come to your house and tell you to get out.*

A few days later Joan told Mom that an officer appeared at her front steps and asked her details about their house—rent, the name of the owner, how many square feet of living space there was, and so on. At the same visitation he wanted to know who owned our house. Joan asked, "Why, you take these houses?"

He answered, "Don't know. Maybe."

"You give us notice," she said she told him.

"Maybe," he answered, after which he left, crossed the street, and went to look at other houses.

Mr. Sheerer, the owner of both our homes, became concerned and came over to tell us Naval officers had told him they were looking for a nearby residence to house some their officers. He said he informed them that we have rental contracts with him and they can't just kick us out. They responded they would find other houses for the Camons and us.

The next day the drama ended. The officer returned and told Joan they had changed their minds. "Take other house across street," he announced.

On Easter Sunday I joined some members of the family at La Salle Chapel for services. The altar was draped in white and the organ played several triumphant hymns celebrating the Resurrection. When I took communion, I felt a spiritual lift that is difficult to describe. I could only call it *spiritual*. At moments like those I was sure I was a true believer. Everything took on a peaceful aura, until we got back on the dusty streets, which were never cleared of garbage. Pyramidal piles of rotting refuse— melon rinds, discarded bones, decaying vegetables, feces, and dead animals littered street corners. As we passed Vito Cruz, the stench steaming from a mountain of garbage some four feet high brought our handkerchiefs to our noses. An old woman dressed in a torn faded *bata* dug through the muck. The head of an infant held in the crook of her arm was covered with flies. When a number of the flies buzzed off, a colony of pustules oozed from the crown of the baby's head.

That scene, combined with the memory of the fall of Bataan two years previous, obliterated any joy I had felt at the Easter Service. *There is nothing to be happy about,* I wrote in my diary, describing the garbage and my feelings of depression about the anniversary of Bataan. *Worst of all, after Easter lunch, Candida told us she must leave for Batangas. Her family needs her help on the farm. Her parents are getting too old to manage the land.*

She packed a few days later. After saying goodbye to Mom, she tried to sneak out to the street to avoid having to say goodbye to the rest of us. I spotted her, holding a bayóng full of possessions, as she swung open the iron gate. I raced after her, losing one of my bakias on the driveway and barely catching up with her.

"Candida, wait!" I shrieked, grabbing on to the green-
flowered dress she wore on her days off.

She turned her head so I wouldn't see her tears. I could hear
the sobs suppressed in her throat. "Oh, Candida," I cried, burying
my face into her shoulder. "You can't leave without saying
goodbye to me!"

She didn't speak. She simply held my hands, curling her
strong brown fingers around mine and nodding her head. Then
pressing her check against mine, she broke away to hail a passing carretela. Within seconds she was carried off. She did not
look back. Through a wash of tears, I watched the carretela grow
smaller and smaller until it faded into the heat waves on Taft
Avenue. The *clip-clop* of the horse's hooves became numbers
she had taught me in Tagalog years ago—*isa, dalawa, tatlo, ap-
at, lima*—counting the years in the decade she had been a part of
my life. I sensed I would never see her again.

X

After we lost Candida, Mom and I took care of the cooking. We hired several house girls to help with the cleaning, but none of them stayed long. One woman stole several pieces of silver cutlery and was fired. Felisa, who was about my age, joined us in May and only stayed for a few months. Our laundry was done by a part-time lavandera. Fortunata had returned to her province months before. I missed her wry sense of humor and seeing her tiny form every afternoon, balancing a basket of ironing on her head. In just a matter of time, we knew we would be washing our own clothes. I was already doing my underwear, and scrubbing the rags I needed every month—a foul job.

We sometimes bathed twice a day so that we would not have to change our clothes, morning and afternoon. Deodorants had disappeared, even from the black market. There was nothing we could do to get rid of the odor of sweat except bathe.

Our most enjoyable time together was in the evenings when we sat on lawn chairs in the garden by the bonga palm and talked under the stars. Bert would be full of news, having just listened to the short-wave radio hidden in the closet. In my mind's eye I can still see him leaning forward, his voice rasping as he tried to keep it as low as he could. In mid-May, he reported progress on the Allied invasion of Italy. Then on June 4 we heard our forces had entered Rome. That night my diary entry read: *Spent the morning practicing, taking care of the chicks and darning clothes that are filled with holes due to so much wear and the*

present harsh soap. At lunch heard that Rome has fallen! I tell
you I felt like I had nervous indigestion and I couldn't sleep my
siesta thinking about it. For more than two weeks Allied forces
were outside the city. According to Japanese news sources, Hit-
ler ordered the evacuation of the city. I got to thinking how many
times Rome has fallen—first, the sack of Rome in 390 B.C., then
the burning of the city in 64 B.C., and so on, through the centu-
ries.

Then on June 6, there was more good news: *Ohh! I'm trying*
to be calm, because right now I feel as if I have worms in my
belly and stones in my mouth! On the six P.M. news from New
Delhi we heard that the Second Front invasion of Europe is on!
Combined Allied navies, planes, and paras carried out the oper-
ation, which began at dawn this morning. The Allies have re-
venged Dunkirk after four years!

The next few weeks brought continued Allied successes. On
June 15, a day before my seventeenth birthday, U.S. bombers
blasted Tokyo, a sure indication that American carriers were in-
filtrating Japanese-held waters.

It rained buckets on June 16, but not until after my birthday
party. Liselotte, Miriam, Carmen, Georgie, and Margie came for
merienda. I wrote: *Today was perfect. I don't think I've been*
happier in all three years of war. The minute I awoke I felt a tin-
gle of excitement. Seventeen. Just imagine! And today—my day.
Mom's present was so lovely. She sewed a red-and-white pina-
fore for me from a peasant skirt she bought in Nice, France, in
1933. She bought a pair of red canvas, rope-soled alpargatas to
match. She also knitted a pair of underpants for me! But the best
present from her was a poem she wrote celebrating my seven-
teenth birthday.

Don and Jim gave me a box of powder and a comb. I felt so
pleased at everything I was tongue-tied. I knew that with all the
remarks and glances my way, I would just cry if I said how much
it all meant to me. Bert said to Mom at the breakfast table, "You

know, she's the most unsophisticated girl of seventeen I've ever known!"

Mom said, "Now, no picking on her on her birthday!" They were all surprised when I took Bert's remark as a compliment.

All the girls—Miriam, Carmen, Georgie, Margie, and Liselotte came to my party this afternoon. We chattered away until teatime, and then everyone just ate. My brothers and cousins ate until they couldn't!

The cake was very nice, though everyone said last year's was better because Mom had made it. I took a number of seconds wishing over the candles. Auntie Teresita said, "Come on, hurry up."

"Wait!" cried someone else, "she must be wishing a combination wish—everything included." I was.

I received two pins, a bag, two pairs of panties, soap, cologne, a book, two pairs of alpargatas, a brassiere, a prayer book, and some money. At six o'clock everyone went home. The girls packed together in a carretela and kissed me good-bye, amidst loud giggles. The rain waited, but by 6:30, it was pouring!

Before I fell asleep I remember thinking Mom had told me that on the night before I was born there was an eclipse of the moon. She thought that made me special. But the poem she wrote for me on my seventeenth birthday demonstrated how really special she thought I was.

> *Dearest daughter of mine,*
> *You know, dear, poetry is not my line,*
> *But I'll do my best,*
> *If you promise not to make it a jest:*
> *On this great day, your birthday,*
> *I wish you all the joy you deserve.*
> *And I'm proud to say*
> *(Though I have kept it—reserve)*
> *That you are the sweetest daughter*

A mother could ever hope to get.
Now please don't let this go to your head!
In this time of war and strife
When it is hard to even keep alive,
You have been a great help:
What with cooking, knitting, darning,
And all that goes with economizing,
You've been "Tops"!
Today you are seventeen.
I pray that next year, when you are eighteen,
All will be cheer.
You know what I mean, dear.

In many ways I wish I could have been more like my mother. Mentally and physically we were different. She was *feet on the ground*, and I was *head in the clouds*. She had a dark, airy quality about her, and I was fair and quiet. My mother had beautiful legs. I'd like to say I inherited them, but mine were diminished by rosier skin inherited from my father, in contrast to hers, which were a light golden-brown. Mom worked around her flowers in culottes, exposing her legs to the sun. I can still picture her in her early thirties during the war, when so much she cared about disappeared from her life; all the more reason why she treasured her orchids. Devotedly, she tended the plants, potted in soft soil and moss, set into wire containers, and hung from the trunks of several coconut trees. The orchids bore the most exotic blooms I had ever seen, except for those cultivated especially in Helen's Flower Shop. Mom's orchids varied in color from gauzy green, to deep lavender, to snow white. When they were in full bloom, they reminded me of butterflies, swaying softly in the afternoon breeze, looking as if they would fly away at any moment.

I often wondered what she thought about while she took time each day to be with her orchids. As I watched her, I told myself I wished I could be more like her, but I knew my interests did not lie close to the earth. Instead, my thoughts turned, when in need of solace, to the abstract, to my writing and my artwork. I could easily imagine painting a picture of one of her plants, either in words or in a drawing.

Ironically, Mom was also good at sketching, as was Bert. She loved to sketch caricatures of familiar faces, whereas Bert often drew imaginary figures, with exaggerated noses, huge ears, or ponderous hips. We laughed at his creations and were encouraged to cultivate our own creative talents.

Another trait of Mom's I admired was her compassion. If someone needed her, she was right there. When my father's mother and father were released on medical passes from camp, they were sent to the Remedios Hospital in the Ermita. Grandad had heart problems. Grannie was all right until she developed a large abscess, resulting from an infection called *anthrax*, on the back of her neck. Mom took care of her every day. She put hot compresses on the huge boil, and took hot soup for them both. It was weeks before my grandmother recovered. Bert never said anything, knowing her kindness to her former in-laws was based simply on the goodness of her heart.

I learned a lot from Mom and Bert. They demonstrated values I would live by for the rest of my life. Had it not been for the war, I might never have personally witnessed their basic personalities and learned what was most important to them. By living closely together, we became so dependent on one another we could not hide our true selves.

A few weeks after my birthday, I went for my piano lesson. Solita had not spoken about the underground letters for a long time, so when she told me she had some news, I held my breath, hoping she would say something positive about it. That thought quickly vanished when I saw the look of disappointment in her brown eyes. Her voice quivered when she said, "The Japs are taking more and more POWs to Japan to work in their coal mines and steel mills. Your Harry is probably on a waiting list at Bilibid Prison. That's where they base them before they ship them out. That's one reason we haven't heard. We've lost all contact. I'm so sorry." She reached for my hand.

"Japan!" I exclaimed. A sense of dread made the hair on the back of my neck prickle. I was sure there would be no hope for him. "Even if Harry makes it to Japan, when the Americans invade the islands, the Japs will kill the POWs."

She could say nothing to comfort me. We both knew of a couple of unmarked Japanese transport ships filled with POWs that had been sunk by U.S. subs. The grapevine was filled with tales of hardship suffered by prisoners working in the mines and mills in Japan. I hung my head. "Forgive me if I can't play today, Solita. I feel sick."

She led me to the sala, where we sat in silence, fanning ourselves with pay-pays. The *clip-clop* of carretelas and the whine of passing trucks came up from the street, and once in awhile, we heard the high cry of a vendor. Solita served glasses of calamansi juice and some rice cookies. I drank the juice but my stomach felt too tight to handle the cookies. "You know," I commented, "every afternoon I sit in our yard by our bignay tree, where I can look out and watch the trucks filled with POWs heading from work to some camp in Pasay. They look terrible, Solita—clothes in tatters, and they are so thin. I keep searching for Harry."

"Have you seen him?" she asked, her voice faintly hopeful.

"Sometimes I think I have, but it must be my imagination. I wonder if I saw him if I would even recognize him."

She sighed heavily. The chair she sat on creaked. "It's hell, isn't it? Everything is falling apart. I hear the commander in Santo Tomás is a monster. The internees are all beginning to starve. God, our troops have got to hurry back!"

"They'd better," I added, "and I hope we live to see it."

XI

On July 22, we harvested a bed of peanuts we had planted. It was such an event I described it in my diary: *We had a surprise today. We harvested our peanut bed and gathered a ganta of peanuts from it. From our own land—a tasty crop of peanuts! We boiled a batch and ate it immediately. A ganta of peanuts costs 40 pesos at the market, so you can bet we ate everything but the shells, and all agreed to plant* maní, *Tagalog for* peanuts, *again next year.*

That same week Liselotte and brother Tim came over to pick berries from our bignay tree—ripe, marble-sized ruby berries that made tasty jam. After we picked, a heavy rain, which had soaked the three of us, let up. Liselotte and I were still perched in the tree when one of us started throwing berries at the other. Soon we were in a crazy berry fight. Standing below us, Tim picked up the bignay fruit as it dropped and slung it back at us. We laughed so hard we almost fell off the tree.

On the first of August we made preparations to celebrate Bert's thirty-fifth birthday. I fashioned a card and wrote a rhyme. Mom made some fudge, using bitter black chocolate she sweetened with raw brown sugar. She used coconut milk because canned cow's milk and fresh carabao milk were no longer available. We cooked half a ham we processed from a pig our neighbors had slaughtered and sold to us.

The next morning, Don, Jim and I dressed Maxie up with a red ribbon, tied the birthday card on his neck, and pushed him into Mom and Bert's room. "Happy birthday!" we chorused. Bert sat up in bed and cried, "Oh-ho!" Lately, he had been edgy, and it was good to hear him laugh.

A couple of weeks after we celebrated Bert's birthday, Manila carried out its first total air defense practice. The radio announced that on August 15 the city would be in a state of alert. No sirens would sound. The state of alert would be in effect until an all clear was given by the radio.

As expected, traffic was stopped on Taft. Not a single carretela, bicycle, or go-cart trafficked the street. Bert said that the U.S. invasion of Guam and other successes in the Pacific were bringing the war closer to us, making the Japs nervous—hence the air defense practice.

During this time my tutor left because we could longer afford her. Mom lost her Spanish students, resulting in the termination of my music lessons. My depression was further deepened by the loss of communication with Harry. There was little to look forward to.

When several soldiers searched our yard in mid-August, I panicked and flushed Harry's letters, which were hidden in the bathroom behind the brick with my diary, down the toilet. My heart knocking against my ribs, I waited for the soldiers to search our house. When they left after poking around the yard, I was inconsolable. How could I have been so quick to destroy letters that meant so much to me? Fear! Fear was making me paranoid. Every time I saw a soldier lingering near our gate, I imagined an imminent search. It had happened before. It could happen again.

I rewrote every word Harry had written from memory. I hid segments of the letters in various locations, so that if one segment were found, it would not make much sense by itself. I hid my diary in a coffee can and buried it under a rock in the duck pen, and I secured bits and pieces of Harry's recreated letters there as well. I was glad I could save what he had written, but the loss of the original letters left me deeply saddened.

I retreated to my room, spending hours staring out the window, when I wasn't writing in my diary. My mother knocked lightly on my door one afternoon. "Why don't you come out and join us? You've been in your room for hours. It's not healthy for you."

"I'm not good company."

Sitting on the bed beside me, she put her arm around my shoulder. "We all know how you are feeling about Harry's letters. No one expects you to act happy, but we'd like for you at least to be with us."

I shook my head. "I feel as if a huge blanket separates me from everyone. It's an unreal feeling—like I'm not really me." I reached up and placed my hand over hers. "Honestly, I don't want to feel this way. I just do, Mom." My voice began to crack.

She stood up and pulled me up with her. "Come on. Let's go sit in the garden and drink some calamansi. We'll talk."

Woodenly, I went along. We drank calamansi juice, which we enjoyed several times a day. Jokingly we called it a tonic. The golf ball size limes grew profusely in our garden. It was a refreshing source of vitamin C and eased the effects of the intense tropical heat. Mom and I talked as we sipped the sweet, iced juice. "You are a smart girl, Doreen," she began. "Part of your problem is that your mind isn't occupied. Since you're no longer studying, you have too much time to sit and imagine all kinds of things. Bert and I feel you should continue with some schooling."

I frowned. "I thought we couldn't afford schooling."

"There's a secretarial course being offered at Santa Scholastica's that is quite reasonable—about half what we were paying for tutoring. I think it would be good for you to attend a couple of classes."

I knew I didn't have a choice. My parents were right. I needed something to occupy my mind. I agreed to enroll in two classes—typing and bookkeeping, provided I could quit if they didn't work out.

The Catholic school was about a mile away from us. Mom or one of the boys walked me to class each day. The nuns welcomed me with reserved smiles. The students, all Filipinas, greeted me as the stranger I was. By the second week, they had tentatively accepted me, and although I couldn't speak more than a few phrases of Tagalog, I could understand more than I could communicate. My classmates switched to English when they chose to. Sister Letticia, my room teacher, was a spry, diminutive woman, who smiled easily. The twinkle in her eyes had the effect of overriding the strict rules she enforced.

I didn't care much for bookkeeping, penciling endless worksheets and ledgers, but I enjoyed typing class. After several weeks I was able to type my diary entries. My accomplishments at school lifted my depression, so that I found I was less paranoid and slept more soundly. Temporarily, I had defied the haunting specters of battle and death.

Air defense exercises took place again before the month of August ended. An announcement was made that the boulevard would be permanently closed. Grandma and I took a last walk on the palm-lined street after church one Sunday. There was military activity going on by the seawall involving tanks, armed trucks, and soldiers. We left quickly.

On August 24, a partial blackout was declared, along with another general state of alert. Searchlights danced all over the sky. What were they expecting?

As military activity accelerated, we noticed the Japanese Navy at the American School was carrying out maneuvers. Their daily shouts could be heard all day long.

Don, who was forever on the lookout for news, told us he was sure Marco, our garbage man, was a guerrillero. The tall, dark Filipino, with gray-green eyes that revealed a mixed ancestral background, confided in Don that he had spied on the Japs at the school and was sure all kinds of guns, ammunition, engine parts and rubber tires were being stored there. When asked what he thought about the large amount of equipment being warehoused, Marco shrugged his shoulders and gave a mysterious half-smile. Intrigued, Don asked him if he was involved with the guerrillas. He did not answer. He jumped over the fence like a leopard, avoiding the deadly sharp bars, and ran down the street, the large tin garbage can bumping on his broad back.

Several days later, two truck tires were stolen from the school. We were not prepared for what happened next. It was just after a breakfast of leftover warm rice, coconut milk and raw sugar, when we were startled by shouts from the street. The chains on our gate clanged heavily. Bert spilled some of his coffee when he set his cup on the table and bolted down the front steps, the rest of us at his heels. "Wait here!" he waved us back. "God knows what the hell they want."

We bunched up on the steps while Bert ran and opened the gate. Four Japanese soldiers and one officer, all bearing pistols, closed in around him. His flushed face appeared above theirs as they moved back toward us. My brothers flanked Mom and me. Bert elbowed his way up to the lower step, the soldiers hissing epithets, on the ground level below him. His lips stretched over his teeth, my stepfather's face became an ugly snarl. I knew that if the Japanese officer waving a gun were to get much closer, Bert would hit him with his right fist, which was clenched so hard his knuckles had turned bone white.

Above the babble and gun-waving, the officer yelled and pointed his pistol right under Bert's nose. "You, you," he sputtered in English, "you stole tire—two tires—from outpost last night!"

Somewhat sobered by hearing the officer speak English, Bert squinted at him "W-what?" he cried in disbelief.

I sagged against Mom. Thank God, Bert had backed away from the officer. I had the same reaction I had experienced when Mom and I were accosted in the early days of the occupation. My chest constricted and my knees knocked. My brothers pressed in against me. I could barely see over their shoulders.

The officer must have been partly convinced by Bert's astounded expression that he might not be guilty of stealing the tires. He turned abruptly and gave a command to his men. Like robots they swarmed around us and shoved us down the steps into the driveway and across the yard to the front fence. I had a sudden image of impending doom, of being executed where we stood, in our own yard, for a crime we knew nothing about.

As soon as they had herded us by the fence, the soldiers formed a menacing ring around us. The officer stood in the center and pointed a stubby finger at the ground. All heads turned downward. Clearly imprinted in the soft mud there appeared two tire marks and two bare footprints, sturdy heels pressed into the earth. "You!" the officer stabbed his index finger into Bert's chest.

That was all it took. Bert exploded "God damn, sonofabitch! If I took your God-dam tires do you think I would leave footprints? Look! I wear shoes!"

Mom pressed in behind Bert and put her hands on his shoulders. "Please, dear, please!"

He heard her pleas, stepped back, and stared at the officer.

"Shoes! Take off shoes," the officer commanded. His eyes narrowed closed.

My God, I thought, he's going to match Bert's foot with the footprint in the mud. Please, don't let them match! They didn't. Bert's feet were far wider and his toes stubbier. "Humph!" cried the officer. He reached for Don, who had already begun to remove his shoes. My brother's feet were longer than the footprint, his heels far narrower. Jim was next. He, too, passed the test. It was clear that none of the feet in our family would match the guilty footprints.

They had no case. The officer waved his men away. They charged down the driveway and out the gate. Bert's ashen face sagged. Mom clutched his arm. The officer waited before he stepped out the gate, his eyes burning with disdain. "Your fault. Fence too low. Must not happen again." He waved his pistol once more before placing it in his holster. He told us his men would return to string barbed wire over the iron bars of our fence, raising it to a full eight feet. The gate would also be rigged with barbed wire, and they would padlock it.

It took them an afternoon to complete the operation. When they were through, they had made us prisoners in our own yard. I hated the sight of that fence. At that time I did not know how significant it would be in the near future.

I thanked my brothers for their protection during the tire incident. They were becoming young men. Almost sixteen, Don was tall and fair, his eyes bluer than ever. Jim, a year younger, had become rangy also, but his rich brown hair and Spanish eyes were in contrast to his brother's, and to mine. Both boys had the same gait, long swinging arms and toes pointed slightly outward. I could spot them a mile down the street. Jim was quieter. Always had been, almost as if he counted on Don to speak for him, but he didn't miss a thing. His eyes scanned everything. Thus it was he who caught Mom in a deception no one expected. After the incident was over, the details of the story were revealed.

Here is what happened: Before sun-up one dewy morning, Jim heard Mom get up and sneak into the garden. Dressed in a pale pink cotton housecoat and slippers, she carried a dented aluminum pail. He watched her bend over, in and out of the vegetable garden, picking up dark, pebble-like objects and putting them into the pail. Snails! He realized they were large, juicy garden snails that had invaded our garden, their yellow and brown shells slithering over the ground, their slimy bodies leaving silver trails all over the vegetables. They were voracious.

Jim watched her fill the pail. As she sneaked back into the house, he returned quietly to his room. All day he wondered what she had done with the snails. At dinnertime, he found out. She served them for supper! After I heard what had happened, I wondered how she had kept a straight face when she told us we were eating mushrooms and tomato sauce over rice!

Jim leaned forward on his elbows. "Where did you get the mushrooms, Mom?"

"Oh, from the market yesterday," she answered, passing the dish around. "Have some, they're delicious."

They smelled good and the fleshy black blobs looked tasty, swimming in rich tomato sauce with onions and garlic. I had a second helping, as did all of us except Jim. He sat glancing up occasionally at Mom and picked at his food. After dinner he asked if he could speak to her alone. They went into the hallway. We could hear him when he confronted her. "Why did you lie, Mom? Those were snails you made us eat!"

At that point we were all straining our ears toward the hallway. When they walked back into the dining room, I could see Mom had been fully chastised. Her head down, her eyes filled with tears, she was blushing noticeably. She let out a quivering sigh. "I'm sorry," she said, "I didn't know how else to make you eat them."

Jim wasn't through. "But Mom, why those snails? We're not starving yet."

Mom's lower lip firmed, "Because there wasn't any meat to serve. I thought it was a good way to get rid of the snails. They're a menace in our garden."

We began to exchange smiles. Jim softened. He touched her shoulder. Our mother leaned up against him. "I'm sorry I lied. I'm worried. Rice is now $550. per sack. Prices are, are . . ."

"It's O.K., Mom," Jim said. "Next time just tell us what's on our plates."

Sitting quietly at the head of the table, Bert could no longer hide his amusement. "I sort of liked the mushrooms fixed that way, or should I say, *Snails à la Maria?*"

I had always had a temper. It flared easily, but soon sputtered out. My brothers had several nicknames for me. One of them was *Psst-Boom!* They often provoked me on purpose just to get my reaction. Deep and lasting rage was an emotion I was unacquainted with until the afternoon when my parents sold our two pet ducks to a friend. I shouldn't have been surprised. Bert had announced that ducks, chickens, and turkeys that were not producing eggs or were getting old and tough must go, either be sold or be eaten. We were running out of corn. The boys were no longer able to buy and sell it on the black market. As food shortages increased, grain for the fowl just wasn't easily available. We were all aware that Donalda and Wobbles were now old, and they hadn't been laying much. I guess I should have been glad they were to be sold, and not to be eaten at our table. But when Mom's friend, Mrs. G., came to get them, I could only watch from my bedroom window and put my hands over my ears to drown out their wild squawking as their feet were tied and they were shoved into a large covered basket. I began to holler hysterically, kicking at the door to my room.

I heard Bert's footsteps before he got to my locked door and began to rap loudly. "What's going on?" he yelled. "Open up. I want to talk to you!"

I felt the blood pounding in my head. "Go away. I hate you!"

"I said, 'open the door!'"

"No!"

My mother's voice suddenly intervened. "Doreen, let us in. We want to explain."

My chest heaving, I paused a moment, then swung the door open and stared belligerently at them. Bert stepped into the room and grabbed me by the shoulders. "Have you lost your mind?"

Mom slipped in beside him and tugged at his arm. "Let her speak."

"Speak, then," he ordered.

His anger unnerved me and triggered more rage. "I hate you for selling my ducks. I'll always hate you!"

He slapped me hard on the side of the face. The blow sent me reeling. I crumpled into the bed, wailing so loudly I didn't hear them leave. I sobbed for what seemed hours. Dinnertime went by and I fell asleep watching the sun fade on the mango tree branch that brushed against my window.

The next morning hunger gnawed at me, but I avoided the family at breakfast. I showered, dressed and went down to the empty duck pen, where I sat and expressed my indignation in my diary. Soft white down feathers had accumulated against the sides of the pen—an unbearable reminder. I brushed up a handful and held them to my nose, sniffing the last of my pet ducks.

Later, I raided the refrigerator and found some leftover rice and a cup of coconut milk I had previously scraped and squeezed. I spent the rest of the day in silence, going about my chores. Bert found me folding laundry when he got home from work. The anger was gone from his eyes. "Let's be reasonable, Fifi. First of all, I'm sorry I slapped you. I lost my temper. You were hysterical. I've never seen you like that."

I felt a hard lump threatening in my throat. I said nothing. He leaned back against the window ledge and sighed heavily. "These are hateful times. We didn't want to sell your ducks. You know that. We just can't feed them. It was the best solution— that, or eating them."

I knew he was right, but I had my pride. In the end I was unable to hold back my tears. I found myself weeping in his arms. "I'm sorry, too," I blubbered. "I loved them so much."

He held me tight. "I know. I know you did. After this is all over, we'll get some new pets. I promise. Come. Let's find Mom. She's been upset."

It wasn't difficult to find Mom. She had been listening outside the door. I could tell by her red, puffy eyes that she had been crying, but a wavering smile revealed her relief that yesterday's rage had given way to a resolution. I vowed I would try to improve my ways and concentrate on my studies and chores. It frightened me to think I could get so overwrought and lose control of my emotions. At the same time the grief I felt at all the losses I had experienced recently fueled a fear of impending doom that had dogged me for months and had made me so vulnerable I crumbled at the slightest crisis. No matter what I did, I was just one step from wanting to run and hide from my own thoughts. On the other hand, the idea that the Americans could actually be at our shores thrilled me beyond description. Looking back, I was in a high state of anxiety, where my responses were exaggerated; where I knew I could lose control because I had just proved I could. More frightening, was realizing my parents were also on edge. Bert had never slapped me in all the years he had been a father to me. All he ever had to do was warn me by giving me a look of disapproval. I knew I must keep a rein on myself if I was going to keep my sanity.

XII

The air defense exercises had become routine. It was no surprise to witness mock dogfights and corresponding ack ack fire. Around 9:15 on the morning of September 21, while I was at Santa Scholastica's concentrating on a bookkeeping exercise, Sister Letticia called roll and led prayers. Behind her large wooden desk, she looked like a little girl, dressed up, play-acting she was a nun. She hardly looked up when the *rat-tat-tat* of machine gun fire began. It wasn't until the urgent whine of planes diving directly overhead blasted in through the windows that we raised our heads from our work in wonderment.

"That sounds real!" the girl next to me cried.

Dozens of heads turned toward the window, where two planes were suddenly visible, firing and zooming at each other, several other fighters crisscrossing behind them. I recognized the red circle of Japan on the wings of one plane and the American star insignia on the other. A low hum reverberated above the dogfight like a menacing growl.

Without warning, dozens of silvery wings glinted in the smoke-streaked sky. Bombers—hundreds of them! Air raid sirens joined the cacophony, as bombs thudded, ack ack tracers exploded, and fighters zoomed about the sky. It was a bizarre combination of sounds that resonated in my chest and stimulated my heartbeat into a wild arrhythmia.

Sister Letticia bolted from her chair, sending a sheaf of papers flying to the floor. Her rosary beads struck the side of her desk as she rushed to the center of the room. She jerked her arms like a frightened penguin. Her voiced pitched high, she cried, "Girls, girls, quick to the hall!"

As she lifted her arms to hold our attention, the sleeves of her habit spread like black wings and she was off, we, trailing helter-skelter behind her. We knew where we were to assemble during a raid, and although our class became mixed up with students rushing out from other classes, we ended up in a designated corner, where we knelt, heads down on the black and white tile floor, our arms over our heads. "Pencils!" Sister shouted. "Rosaries!"

Most of us had already jammed pencils between our teeth, but I found it impossible to keep my head down and recite the rosary. A perfect view of the sky was visible from a small square window above me. Transfixed, I watched a sea of bombers in formation fly over like so many silver fish lined up, row after row, the steady hum of their engines buzzing a greeting. Americans! Americans, finally here to liberate us!

Bombs rained down, some falling so close, probably on Nichols Field and the Port Area docks, that the glass on the window trembled, bowed, and threatened to blow out from the pressure. A large cathedral glass window across the hall rattled and shattered, sending bits of colored glass splintering to the floor. Several students gasped and pushed me into the corner, where a cactus plant began to poke its spikes at my back. "Ouch! Don't crowd!" I cried, but no one heard or paid attention, Sister Letticia least of all. She was praying so earnestly I could hear her *Hail Marys* above the exploding sky. Many of the students responded in chorus.

The raid continued for about an hour, as wave after wave, which we found out later were carrier-based bombers, dropped hundreds of bombs on military installations, as protective wings of fighters zigzagged under them engaged in deadly dogfights. For me the formations looked like silver angels, avengers on a long wished-for mission.

Civilians had crowded into the school for shelter. Some of them were nursing shrapnel wounds and others, cuts from broken glass. As the bombers withdrew, their drones growing more and more faint, the antiaircraft guns finally fell silent, and the all clear sounded a weak, wailing anti-climax.

The hallway became a hornet's nest. A mixture of Tagalog, English, and Spanish clashed and rose to a babble. One of my classmates tugged at my arm. "You're bleeding. It's shrapnel!"

I glanced down and saw a trickle of blood running down my forearm. Touching the sore spot, I started to laugh. "Shrapnel from *that!*" I pointed to the cactus. My classmate burst out in nervous laughter. Her eyes sparkled and she leaned over and whispered. "Wasn't the raid wonderful?"

"Oh, yes!" I exclaimed.

Not wonderful was the sight of a wounded child lying on a stretcher just inside the front door. I couldn't take my eyes off her tiny round face, pale as milk, under crude, bloodstained bandages wound around her head. Sister Letticia put her hand on my arm. "Come on, I'll walk you home," she said, as she gathered together several of us who lived on Taft Avenue.

We proceeded cautiously, stepping over mounds of glass from broken windows. We looked right and left, afraid the military might be stopping people in the streets. There were several trucks loaded with soldiers at the entrance of the American school. None of them paid attention as we walked by on the other side of the street. Sister Letticia dropped me off at our gate. She squeezed my hands. "God Bless you, child. We'll let you know about school."

Mom came flying down the driveway. "Doreen! You're all right. Oh, my God, thank you, Sister," she cried, hugging me as if she had feared she would never see me again. We gave Sister, who was already on her way, a quick wave and ran up to the house. I showed Mom my wound. We both laughed over it, and then she pointed out the window and said, "Look, we lost a branch from the mango tree. Must have been shrapnel. Oh, and

Jim got a cut on his head as he was running down the driveway, but it's just surface."

We never did find shrapnel or whatever it was that cut through the mango tree branch. Don came in from the market, where he told us he had spent the raid lying in a ditch along with discarded fish entrails. "I need a shower!" he exclaimed.

"Phew!" we chorused.

Adding to our excitement, two more air raids took place that afternoon.

That night Bert told us the short-wave radio described the air raid, calling it a major hit on Luzon. For us it proved planes were now within striking distance, probably from carriers. It must have been the case, for the next day, we were bombed again. They blasted the airfields, the piers, and the Japanese embassy.

In the next few weeks the euphoria I felt during the two raids turned to apprehension, as it became clear the bombing was only a prelude. There were no more raids. What would happen when the real offensive began? The compulsive fears of a burning, bombed-out city returned, stronger than ever.

When the Japanese first entered Manila, I described I felt like a prisoner in a windowless room. That feeling prevailed, only now there was no place to go except further inward, into the labyrinth of my imagination. In that unsure territory, I fought a mental battle staged in a holocaust, where, helpless, I confronted bloody images and was eventually killed. I was sure that when the real battle came I would die. Nothing I said or did relieved me of that obsession. Depression, like a black, descending curtain suffocated me.

Crippled by my obsession, I don't know how I managed to do my chores. My hands and feet felt like lead. My mind was fuzzy, as if a veil separated my inner and outer worlds. Which was the true reality?

I sensed that Mom, Bert, and my brothers knew I wasn't myself. They didn't mention it, but they acted protectively, their eyes followed me and they were quick to come to my aid. In some ways their pain must have been deeper than mine. There was nothing they could do except show me, in their hesitant and silent way, that they cared.

My dependence on prayer vanished. No matter how much I prayed, the thoughts of death persisted. When I confessed my sins to Father Kelly I tried to explain my obsession. His reaction only fueled my dilemma. "Only God knows when we will die, child. It's a sin to second-guess God."

God's rage on my hands, I gave up, and let the obsession take over. What was the worst that could happen? In a strange paradox, when the bombers came over, as they began to do again in October, any vision I had about being hit by a stray bullet or a piece of shrapnel slowly dissipated. Did that reality serve as an antidote for my fears? Mom had to yell for me to get into the shelter when I was slow to respond. During one of the raids, she looked at me in disbelief and couldn't resist saying, "If you're so afraid of dying, you'd better come in the shelter!"

In October, after the landings on the island of Leyte, just south of Luzon, my anxiety peaked. On the morning of the 24th, while we were in the shelter, I half-dozed, my head against the packed dirt of the inside wall. In what I can only describe as a waking dream, I had a vision of a young blond man lying suspended on a bed of golden wheat, a purple robe over his body. His eyes were closed, his face peaceful, his hair as golden as the field of wheat. Harry! It's Harry, I said to myself, mesmerized by the gentle swaying of the grain cradling his body. *He's dead! He must be dead!*

"Doreen, wake up, the raid is over!" It was Mom nudging me.

"Mom, I had the most amazing vision," I said, and began to describe in detail what had appeared like a Technicolor movie in my mind. I could tell she thought it was another fantasy, but she looked at me with a look of patience that had become familiar. "It's a dream, dear. Just think of it as a dream."

It's difficult to explain how the vision was a clear message to me that Harry was dead. The very truth of it relieved the anxiety that had haunted me for months. I knew. I found I could deal with the reality. It was valid. It gave me a faith in myself that had been shattered by the uncertainty of an obsessive anxiety. The meanderings of my imagination began to give way to more solid ground. Along with it came a deep, hollow sense of loss, and I was able to cry as I had not cried for weeks. The cold fist that gripped my stomach loosened. I knew I would be able to face whatever lay ahead, bloodbath and all—that I might die, we might all die, was justified. It had become as real as Harry's death scene. I could now finally face the truth of war. Synonymous with death, I could not run from it.

XIII

The arrival of Uncle Tito, Aunt Rosemary, Patricia and Posy in November put the final touches on my recovery. The Japanese took over their house, and despite promises to find them another, they threw them out. Wearing the clothes on their backs, lugging several boxes and bayóngs, in which they had quickly packed their possessions, and struggling with a couple of mattresses and Posy's crib, they arrived at our doorstep. We welcomed them. I gave up my room and moved in with Mom and Bert, while the four of them squeezed into my room. Uncle Tito slept on a cot, Aunt Rosemary and Patricia on mattresses on the floor, and Posy in her crib, tightly pushed up against the wall.

As soon as they arrived, I became involved in the care of my two cousins, Patricia, aged seven, and Posy, barely four. They followed me everywhere, asked me endless questions and begged me to join in their games. Becoming involved with them kept me from concentrating on myself. We made paper dolls. I helped them with their baths, combed and braided their hair, and we planted seeds in the garden and watched them grow.

Patricia was quick and sharp. She was aware of all that went on in the household. She carried tales from one to the other, engaging our laughter as she exaggerated what she had heard. We called her *the town crier*. Posy, on the other hand, was pale and quiet. She lacked her older sister's vigor and clung to her mother.

I liked my aunt and uncle. They were relaxed and showed an interest in me. They were so relaxed that, in retrospect, I can call them downright messy. My old room often looked like a typhoon had hit it. On the good side, they faced problems with calm and good humor. At times this irritated Mom who was organized and painstaking in carrying out household chores. However, she and Aunt Rosemary had their good times after the day's work was done and they sat and chatted in the sala, sipping the last of a bottle of Scotch Uncle Tito had brought.

Aunt Rosemary loved to draw and was good at it. I copied her scenes of tropical paradise, complete with young ladies languishing by laden coconut trees set against pastel sunsets. She also liked to sing and she taught me the lyrics of her favorite tunes. I joined her with fervor when she lifted her voice in a mellow alto—*Just a song at twilight when the lights are low . . .*

Life with her, Uncle Tito, and the girls was a rich experience for me. It offered a much-needed distraction.

The air raids increased after the Leyte landings. When the Japanese Navy suffered defeat in the Battle of Leyte Gulf, more and more bombers covered our skies. A passageway to northern Luzon had been clearly opened. Meanwhile, on the European front, the British landed in Greece and took over Athens. Brussels was liberated and the Russians penetrated into Germany. In December, the Battle of the Bulge began in Europe, and U.S. landings in Mindoro, a neighboring island to Luzon, took place.

Our shelter became a second home, where we stored blankets and pillows and set up a kalan for emergency cooking. We kept a supply of rice, mongo beans, first aid items, and an extra filter for our water dispenser—a round ceramic container, twelve inches in diameter, which housed a porous cone to filter the water, and had a small, attached faucet for pouring. Every corner of the shelter was filled with supplies, forcing us to squeeze, shoulder to shoulder, during raids. We put up with the crowded conditions because we had no choice. Frequent drills on how best to go in and out of the shelter became routine. Our biggest problem was the girls. They became restless in the dark, narrow confines of the covered trench and cried and fussed until we had to bribe them with promises on what we would do when the raids were over.

We had bad news from Santo Tomás. Uncle Pepe tried to get food to Aunt Lolita but was turned away by the guards. The sight of gray-faced, starving civilian prisoners of war, their ribs protruding and their bellies distended, had been too much for him and he came over to vent his feelings. "No sight of Lolita. God knows how they are. By the look of those I saw peering through the fence like convicts, I hate to think of what she's going through." He rolled up one cigarette after another, his hand shaking as he puffed so hard I had to move away.

I said a silent prayer for those in camp. I tried to envision how my aunt, my father, or Marcia and my friends might look— emaciated and dying of hunger. When Uncle Pepe mentioned several people who had died of starvation, including the parents of Bernard and Curtis Brooks, former twin classmates, I shuddered and turned away.

Our battle to store food continued with more and more deliberation as a bleak Christmas loomed ahead. We were living on rations of mongo beans, rice, and available produce from our garden. The price of rice per sack had escalated to over 600 pesos. Only a few of our chickens remained. We had eaten all the old hens and roosters and many of the pigeons. The two turkeys, Gulliver and Lilliput, would be next. The fowl were mostly on their own, foraging in the yard and living on a few rice scraps, as were our dogs. Poor Sheba had died from old age and malnutrition. Maxie and Skippy were so thin we could count their ribs. We saved whatever we could from our plates and doctored the scraps with garlic to control intestinal worms.

There were fewer gifts than ever Christmas, 1944. I made some pipe-cleaner dolls for Patricia and Posy. Uncle Tito carved some whistles for them fashioned from bamboo reeds. We cooked bibingka, using the milk from two coconuts, raw sugar and eggs from one or two younger hens. The recipe included baking soda, which we had carefully horded, and butter, for which we substituted coconut oil. I don't know how we didn't get more bouts of diarrhea than we did. Coconuts are a strong laxative.

On Christmas Eve, Uncle Tito and Bert surprised us by cutting down a large branch from the bamboo clump and setting it into a pot supported by enough dirt to hold it upright. When Uncle brought out several sheets of white wrapping paper, the boys and I exchanged puzzled glances. Patricia spoke up first, "What's that for, Daddy?"

He smiled. His brown mustache quivered and his eyes, which were the color of bittersweet chocolate, danced, setting off crows' feet, which edged his temples. "You'll see, little Daba," he said, using his pet name for her.

It wasn't long before he folded together squares of paper he had cut, manipulating them, as if by magic, into white origami cranes. "It's easy. Let's all make them," he said.

I had made origami birds before, but following his instructions, I found I could turn out four or five in a short time. By then, it was dark outdoors. Dark purple streaks reflected what remained of the sunset. Familiar cricket song came through the windows.

We lit a couple of candles we had saved for the nativity set on the buffet. Candlelight sculpted our faces, softening hard lines. Patricia's honey-colored hair fell over her forehead while she concentrated feverishly on a crane that defied her small fingers. Posy sat and toyed with her square of paper and hummed to herself. Don and Jim raced to see who could make the most cranes the fastest. Mom and Bert exchanged amused glances. I recognized their mysterious exchange, which communicated a secret understanding between them, and which I had long ago stopped trying to decode.

Aunt Rosemary decided she would color the eyes of her cranes with red crayon. Uncle Tito smiled all the while, his wizard fingers moving in and out of the folds of paper.

Using needles and white thread, we attached some fifty or sixty paper cranes to the ethereal, leafy, green bamboo branch.

When we were finished, we stood back and chorused, "Ohh, and ahh!" In the dancing candlelight, the cranes appeared to be in flight. Air in the room moved them just enough to add to the illusion. I felt my heart surge with a joy similar to that I had experienced when Bert lit one hundred candles on our first Christmas tree. The magic wrought by our hands lit up our bamboo Christmas tree. The paper cranes seemed powered by the same pure white candlelight of that Christmas in 1935. If I closed my eyes, I could envision the dancing cranes as clearly as I could see the hundred candles on the Baguio pine on Peñafrancia Street. I would carry that memory with me the rest of my life, as surely as I carried it to light the blackest days of early 1945.

January 7—Today was another air-raid day. At 3:30 P.M. some 13 fighters repeated a beautiful dive on Nichols Field. Jim was just missed by a small piece of shrapnel when he left the shelter too soon. I wish he wouldn't do that. Honestly, this shelter business of going in and out gets exasperating. The boys insist on coming out before the all clear, and Patricia and Posy get so restless they cry and fuss endlessly. No fun when explosions add to their chorus.

January 10—Bert found out today there would be no more office during the duration of hostilities, according to management. Curfew is now enforced from 9 P.M. to 5 A.M., with blackout strictly enforced. Taft is pitch black and there's no sound except for trucks going by and an occasional shout from a soldier. Once in a while shots ring out, and we know someone has violated curfew.

Heard that the J's are mining parts of the Ermita, the bridges across the Pasig, and main roads into the city. Right in front of our house they are beginning to construct tank barricades, using slanted cement pillars. The worst of it is they are picking up civilians and forcing them to work on their projects. It's best to stay home.

This evening, just minutes after I started to write this entry, we heard the most amazing news in the history of three years of

*war—American forces landed on Lingayen Gulf yesterday. They
are some 200 kilometers from Manila! Hallelujah!*

During the following week most of the local markets shut
down. Libertad Market remained open, but produce was scarce
and priced so high it was useless to try to buy anything. When it
was certain there would be no change, Bert decided that before
everything was gone we should spend the 1,000 pesos he saved
for that kind of emergency. When not inflated, 1000 pesos was
equivalent to $500. We bought five kilos of carabao meat—that
was all! We had not eaten meat in a while and immediately
cooked up half and salted and dried the other half. It was clear
we would have to live strictly on reserves of rice, mongo, and
our garden vegetables. After that, we would eat the few fowl left,
which were scrawny and ailing, and dig up the case of corn beef
buried by the shelter. We figured we had enough rice to last
through mid-February if we were careful, plus five gantas of
mongo, some red beans and a garden full of snails! The snails
were not long for this world. If the fowl didn't eat them, we
would!

Every day we watched soldiers stopping traffic, confiscating
carretelas, pushcarts and bicycles—anything that moved. They
came to the house and demanded to know if we had any vehicles. They marched around the yard but didn't find the bikes
hidden behind the bamboo. One of the soldiers looked comical in
leggings made from blue neckties! Were they that badly off?

In mid-January, I met a Swedish girl and her sister who had
moved into the Perez-Rubio apartments about a block away on
Taft. Ulla Greiffe was fifteen, tall and copper-haired—quite
beautiful. Her sister, Birgitta, was eleven, blonde, pug-nosed,
and full of mischief. We decided we would invite them and some
of the boys from the apartment to join us for a game of badminton. It felt good to have a new friend close by. It was too dangerous to travel to the Ermita to visit Liselotte, Carmen and Miriam.
Georgie and Margie had gone back to camp.

*January 15—A clear, sunny day. Ulla, her sister, and the
Romero Salas brothers, plus their friend Porky, all from the*

apartments, helped Don, Jim and me set up a fine badminton net. We refurbished some old shuttlecocks with fowl feathers. We played five games. I found myself totally distracted. The boys teased the girls, and we didn't care who won, just that we were having a good time.

While we played, a false air raid siren blasted. We paid no attention. Good thing it wasn't real. We would have ignored it. Later on we heard gunfire. Don interrupted a game to check. He returned, saying the J's were shooting at Filipino looters, who were breaking into an empty house down the street, stealing furniture, doors, and whole windows. They were even tearing out the floors to sell as firewood.

Diary entries continued to detail our lives, which were a combination of fear and folly. As hundreds of evacuees from the north passed our gate in bedraggled lines, carrying their pitiful possessions and pulling exhausted children by the hand, Ulla, the boys, and I played badminton, in between runs to the air raid shelter, as if our very lives depended on the games. When we wore out shuttlecocks, we sat on the grass and played Truth or Consequences: One of my consequences was to sing a ridiculous song; Billy had to kiss Skippy on the nose, and Ulla had to turn five somersaults—all this, while the sirens shrilled, and evacuees walked wearily by our gate.

If circumstances could become more incongruous, they did: One afternoon a young soldier on the street motioned Don to the fence. He was shorter than my brother by a head, but looked to be about the same age. A wry smile on his face, he handed Don a piece of wrapped candy. Don nodded his thanks and was about to put the item in his pocket when the soldier motioned for him to eat it. Not sure what the soldier would do, Don slowly unwrapped the candy and reluctantly put it in his mouth. When he bit down, cod liver oil squirted into his mouth! He gagged and spat it out. The soldier laughed hilariously, stamping his feet on the ground. Don managed to keep a straight face. He turned and walked back to the house, his fists clenched at his side.

Change became constant. The Japanese limited traffic on the bridges. People had to ride bancas to get across the Pasig. There were numerous accidents in overcrowded, unsteady bancas. Uncle Ovidio and Aunt Teresita were forced to move to the Tabacalera factory when Uncle, without available transportation, had to walk too far to get to work. To make the move they had to rent pushcarts and walk across the city, pushing their possessions in the loaded carts. Aunt Blanca, Dickie and Steffie joined them. It was getting to be too much for them at Uncle Pepe's. Uncle Pepe had run out of money—too many people to feed!

General Krueger's Sixth Army, which had landed on Lingayen Gulf, continued to push down Luzon, headed for Manila. They were twelve miles from Tarlac, where the first POW camps were located after the Death March, about sixty or so miles from Manila. Other landings were made, including one on Subic Bay, also headed for Manila.

In the meantime, inflation got more and more out of hand: a chicken was worth 2,000 pesos; a kilo of pork was 850 pesos; rice, 550 pesos for one ganta; sugar, 800 pesos a kilo. Japanese Mickey Mouse pesos were practically worthless—the exchange was 90 Mickey Mouse to one Philippine peso! Practically no genuine pesos remained in circulation.

January 21, Sunday—This evening we were all knocked dizzy for a split second when a terrific explosion occurred. My, how strong it was, and the way our ears buzzed! We immediately ran downstairs. A few seconds later the sky was lit up and a second thundering blast followed. Downstairs, under the house, we could feel the wind slish by. We counted four seconds between the blasts. Uncle Tito said he thinks some gas tanks must have exploded near by. I am beginning to feel like a war correspondent as I report all these happenings.

January 25, Thursday—Everyone is wondering whether or not there will be street fighting in Manila. As the advance of the American forces penetrates deeper into the plains of southern Tarlac, the situation looks more and more obvious. They are heading straight for Manila! The most talked about question is when they will approach this area, and how will it be? Will there be awful fighting? Will there be just a few hostilities in the outskirts, or will they just march in like the Japs did? My feeling is that there will be a big battle, just as I envision it in my worst imaginings, only now it doesn't frighten me quite like it did. As it gets closer, I think I can face it.

American planes are continually bombing Cavite Naval Base, turning it into a raging inferno. They also drop endless bombs on Corregidor and Bataan. Many are of the opinion that a landing will be made in one of these locations.

The tank barriers the military are putting up outside our house on Taft are so cumbersome they are beginning to totally block the street. The slanted cement barriers are all facing south. Why south? Will an attack come from that direction? Who knows? There are only small spaces left for pedestrians to walk through.

The Navy continues to occupy the school behind us. An officer came by today and told our neighbors, the Camons, they plan to blow up their house and put a gun emplacement there. Imagine the debris! We are only 40 meters away from their fence. It seems we are surrounded. Kamikaze pilots occupy the apartment compound directly to the south of us. At night we hear them chanting before they make their final missions—eerie, gutwrenching wails. By dawn the chanting stops and we know they have left for their date with death. I have seen some of their boyish faces peering out the windows.

In the last days of January, the Navy decided they would not blow up our neighbor's house. In the meantime, American forces kept bearing down toward us. They were 30 miles from us, according to our hidden radio. Other landings were made, including one in Batangas. I hoped Candida was about to be liberated.

On February 1, I wrote a poem and shared it with Mom, who said she agreed with its fearful questions, but felt the poem ended on a positive note. I didn't quite agree.

IT'S FEBRUARY AGAIN

Must I write all o'er again,
about hopes we have on you,
about the same old stuff—our liberation
coming true?

Must I once again remember
that another month has flown;
that we still are striving meagerly,
O' well, we might have known.

But here, I'm kind of hasty,
your "29" may bring a lot—
happiness and food—why
the battle may be fought.

At least I am not greeting you
from forty-three or four;
it makes me awfully glad
those dark days are no more.

O' Feb., you have me frightened!
What will you chance to bring—
bombs, shells, terrific fighting,
and all that sort of thing?

If you could only answer,
I'll bet you'd smile and say,
"Such questions, child, you ask me,
you'll see, my dear, you'll see!"

The first week of February brought more blasting throughout the city. Houses around us were dynamited. Artillery and bombs echoed closer and closer. Because we were incommunicado, as electricity, gas, and water were shut off, we did not know that a contingent of American tanks and soldiers in a surprise attack had crashed through the gates of Santo Tomás and liberated the camp on February 3! Later, we would find out they were from the First Cavalry Division and the 44th Tank Battalion. They had raced down on a suicide run to free the camp. We also couldn't know that Manila was slowly being surrounded by the First Cavalry coming from the north; the Thirty-Seventh Infantry from the east; and the Eleventh Airborne from the south.

Also not known to us was news that General Yamashita had retreated to the northern mountains around Baguio, where he planned to battle the Americans with what was left of his forces. He gave Rear Admiral Marine Commander Sanji Iwabuchi, in charge of the Manila Naval Defense force, orders to declare Manila an open city. Iwabuchi defied his superior's orders and chose to face the surrounding Americans in a last-ditch-stand. His strategy included burning and blowing up the city, killing as many civilians as possible in a final bloodbath—a fight to the death.

I thank God we didn't know what we were in for, as machine gunning, revolver shots, heavy artillery and exploding gasoline and oil tanks were heard in an insane cacophony throughout Manila. No one slept much on the nights of February 4, 5 and 6. We finally decided to move down to the dirt basement, with our petate mats as bedding, foodstuff, and kalans. We watched through the slats of the basement walls while irregular, bedraggled lines of sick and wounded Japanese soldiers trudged by on Taft. We did not know where they were headed, or why. Later we learned they were being marched to the heart of the city to join in the final battle.

I can't recall on which afternoon in that chaotic first week of February Don, Jim and I missed being killed by an antiaircraft shell that fell in our yard as we observed the sun, shrouded by fiery black smoke, and looking more like a strange orange-red moon setting in the sky. We didn't see the shell coming, but were blinded by its fireball and deafened by its blast when it burst in the middle of our vegetable garden, knocking us off our feet. I guess we were far enough away to miss the spray of shrapnel, which cut off some leaves from suckling banana trees and lopped off a few unripe tomatoes. From the jagged hole of the explosion, Don and Jim dug out a large shell fragment, about five inches long, with a four-inch diameter across its base. We were lucky that part of the missile had not exploded.

That blast was a prelude to the fireworks that went up later when the Japanese ammunition dump in front of Ulla's apartment blew up. It was dark by then. The sky had become a Fourth of July spectacle of red, gold, orange, and white fireworks. The smoke that followed was black and suffocating. Ulla's father, Mr. Greiffe, came running over with a pushcart full of their belongings. An hour later when he saw the fires caused by the explosion subsiding, he took the cart back. We helped him push it, just as a convoy of trucks, fully camouflaged, raced by. At the same moment, a lone American fighter swooped down and strafed the convoy, sending us flying back into our yard. We wondered how in the world the plane had spotted the trucks.

The fires spread and climbed higher by the hour. *At sunset, February 5, we saw a sight we'll remember for the rest of our lives. The entire horizon, from east to west, was covered with billowing smoke—the most beautiful smoke I have ever seen. It looked like rolling cotton candy, icing, or meringue. The mass changed from light to bright pink. Then it turned custard yellow, looking as if it could be eaten! At dusk we saw the lower horizon transformed into a shade of deep blood red. As the sky darkened, Manila to the north and east became an inferno. Explosion after explosion added to the conflagration, making the fire bigger and brighter. We got tired and eventually went to bed under the house, all except for Mom who was too nervous to sleep. She reported the fires got so bright in the middle of the night they made tall shadows in the yard.*

Next morning I got up and helped Mom light the kalans for breakfast. I felt stiff from having slept on the ground. I kept picking out stones that poked through my petate mat. My head ached from the concussion—the pressure of each explosion thundered in through my mouth and ears but seemed to be blocked inside my head. Shivering from the early morning chill, I stood as close to my mother as I could. She put an arm around me, but said nothing. What was there to say while we waited for more fires to overtake the city, more shells, and more bombs?

Skippy and Maxie whimpered close to our heels. They were frightened and hungry but had to wait for scraps from the rice pot. Don and Jim joined us by the kalans to warm their hands by the coals. They would have to kill one of our starving hens for chicken soup that night. The meat would be tough. I hated the sight of blood spurting from the necks of the chickens, and was glad I didn't have to kill them. I couldn't have.

Patricia and Posy broke our silence, and soon all of us waited for breakfast as if it were our last meal. What a sorry lot we were—uncombed, unwashed, wearing clothes that should have been in the laundry. We cleaned our bowls of every grain of rice porridge. Each day there was less and less raw sugar to put on it. Since I liked rice plain, I didn't really mind if it tasted bland and soupy.

A worn-out sun rose, still obscured by fiery clouds, still looking like a crimson moon. We were guarding our possessions in a large pushcart in case we had to flee. Filipino looters broke into the abandoned Japanese business compound across the street and stole everything—from furniture to toilet paper; from golf clubs to mattresses; from tools to goldfish, still sloshing around in bowls. They even lifted the floorboards and carried them away by the armload. Some passing soldiers shot at them, but it wasn't long before they resumed their looting. Again, the soldiers returned and finally caught some of the thieves, and tied them up. When they left to catch more looters, those they had tied up freed themselves and ran away. Bert and Uncle Tito hid behind our fence and watched. They said they'd never seen any one run as fast as the Filipinos who got away. We all had a sour laugh over the incident. I wondered what happened to the poor gold-fish!

We began to hear a new kind of detonation. It sounded like balls rolling down a bowling alley, but a hundred times louder, almost like steady claps of thunder. We couldn't figure out what it was. At the same time U.S. planes kept coming over—B24s and fighters. Ack-Ack fire chased after them. It was difficult to tell when machine guns rattled, just who was doing the shooting!

A string of Filipinos dressed in full U.S. army uniforms, who marched unexpectedly by our gate was a disconcerting sight. They must have been *Sakdalistas*—collaborators! No war movie I had ever seen equaled the bizarre pandemonium we were wit-nessing.

I wrote: *Everything is blowing up around us, yet we don't know what is happening. The suspense is unbearable. What will happen next? Our nerves are so taut we hardly speak to one an-other, not sure how our emotions will express themselves. Mom wears a permanent frown on her pallid face. I don't think she sleeps more than a couple of hours a night. Bert growls at every little thing. He yells at the boys for not taking shelter, even when he doesn't himself. He's harder on Don. I suppose because he's older. Uncle Tito's jokes fall flat. Not even Aunt Rosemary laughs. And the dogs are such pests. They cower and hunker so close to us we often stumble over them. They detest the explo-sions more than we do.*

February 8—Mom stays up most of the night now. She is like a guardian angel while we all try to get a few winks lying on the hard ground, our ears deafened by the booming shells and fiery explosions that shake the house on top of us worse than an earthquake. When I open my eyes in between short naps, it is only to see wild shadows from the fires casting huge ghostly forms. We all look like corpses, shrouded in sheets as we try to get some sleep. When it gets too bad, we take refuge in the shel-ter, where we have to sleep sitting up.

We've figured out the pattern the shells make. If a shell is heard going whee-boom, *it's coming toward us; if we hear* boom-whee, *then it's going away from us. We hear both patterns, coming and going. We figure the Americans are firing in, and the Japs are firing out.*

At 6 P.M. on the 8th, I stood on the wide ledge of Mom and Bert's bedroom window, watching the fire bellow. It shot up with each explosion in rolling vermillion clouds, embers flying in all directions. One of the blasts was so near, the house rocked and nearly knocked me off my perch on the window.

Most amazing—in the midst of all the chaos, my brothers found some mudfish in the well we dug months ago to provide water for the garden. We had begun taking water from it for ourselves. It was brackish and muddy, but cleared when we passed it through our filter. As they dipped deeper into the well to access the water, they brought up the fish. Long, whiskered creatures with ferocious eyes, they fished them out and put them over the kalan for a delicious meal. I was reminded of the lapu lapu, which I am certain must be their very close relatives, but no matter, we ate them without reserve. As we ate, we talked about the fires, which we were pretty sure had been set by the Japanese. They wanted to leave nothing behind and to cover up their retreat as the Yanks closed in. Flames ringed the entire city. There were jarring blasts from the direction of the Rizal Stadium, as well as from the Singalong area, where Santa Scholastica was located, and where there was a big munitions dump. On February 10, I continued to describe our lives in the midst of a holocaust and imminent battle: *I guess I'm not going to have another bath until the Americans are in. We have the wells in use so constantly that the mud can't help being stirred up. It makes the water so dirty it has to go through the filter several times, and is then saved for cooking. The cleanest part is kept for drinking. Even then, it tastes salty because we are so close to the bay. I am beginning to smell terrible! So is everyone else.*

We spent all afternoon carrying clothing, bedding, foodstuffs, and portable pieces of furniture—Mom's soapstone desk with the beautiful inlaid figures, the narra dining table and chairs, and a few other items. By dinnertime, the pushcart was full and the yard was littered with furniture.

Mom and I began to take suitcases and bayóng bags to the pushcart we parked in front of the bonga palm. We leaned against the cart for several moments, commenting on the fires, when we were startled by a loud ping *and felt the cart shake. Someone from the street had taken a shot at us, had missed, and hit the pushcart! Never saw who it was. We ran under the house, using the back way.*

At that point, Bert and Uncle Tito climbed over the south fence to get information from some people from nearby residences. They were told the Japs are intentionally using gasoline to set houses and apartments afire, and then shooting the residents as they run out! "Go back and stay hidden. Stay away from your house!" one of the neighbors warned.

The shot that struck our pushcart must have come from a soldier watching us from the street. Three more soldiers came to the gate shortly after dusk, and jabbering loudly, poked their rifles at the big Navy padlock placed there earlier by their counterparts at the school. In reflected firelight, they looked like figures from Dante's inferno, anger burning on their gargoyle faces, their guttural shouts echoing nightmarishly. "Stay out of sight!" Bert warned, crunching low beside us, shielded by the bonga palm and the loaded pushcart.

We saw the soldiers were carrying nambu, *woodpecker machine guns. Shouts from the street suddenly distracted them. They turned and ran. Seconds later, we heard a spray of bullets, followed by shrill cries.*

Uncle Tito, usually ready with a quip or joke, was dead serious when he cried, "We're trapped. We'll die like rats if they don't get here soon!" His face was drawn, his voice shaky.

"Shhh," Mom tried to calm him. "We aren't going to die. We'll stay put and wait right here."

I could see both points of view. We could run or we could stay where we were and face the consequences. I agreed more with Mom. At least we had a shelter in our yard, which was far enough away from the house to distance us if it should catch fire. On the streets we would face the murdering soldiers and would have no clear path to safety. Jumping into the school compound would obviously be suicidal.

"We'll stay," Bert announced. His face, too, bore enormous strain. His skin was gray, and his copper-brown hair was matted with sweat and grime. He appeared much older than his thirty-six years.

Patricia, who had her head on my lap looked up at me. "Will we be O.K.?" she asked. I felt a pang of sadness as I gazed back at her small dirty face. "Yes, we'll be O.K.," I mumbled. What else could I tell her?

I retreated to the shelter with the girls. At 4 A.M. we awoke to more pandemonium. Bert, Uncle Tito and the boys were yelling. "Come out! Come out!" We bolted out of the shelter. God in heaven, we were faced with an avalanching inferno! The houses next to the Mitsui business compound, the Miranda house on the side of the Mitsui, all the houses along Menlo Street west of us, and the entire apartment complex to the south, all were blazing and roaring toward us!

For some crazy reason Bert and Uncle Tito ran back up to the house to bring out a last minute item before the fire licked into the pantry and the kitchen. I must have been out of my mind to suddenly remember a jar of coconut milk I had prepared and forgotten to bring down earlier. Astounding myself, I ran up the stairs, passing Bert and Uncle Tito who were running back out. I raced through the living room, head lowered, my hands over my nose and mouth, and paused for a second to watch the mabolo tree torch up like a giant candle, its round, malodorous fruit sizzling and thudding on the ground. Fascinated, I stood in the kitchen, bright as daylight, and for a second or two I couldn't move. Then I heard Bert's voice. "Doreen, Doreen, get out of there!"

Powered by nerves and excitement, I stopped only one more time before bolting down the stairs. I stared momentarily at my piano, knowing it would soon be reduced to cinders in a funeral pyre. A sharp pain twisted in my chest. "What the hell are you doing? Get down here!" It was Bert again.

This time I didn't stop running until I joined my family, all of them standing like zombies staring up into the flames, and not moving until Tito yelled out, "Move all the stuff that's too close to the house—quick!"

We ran around like ants whose nest has been set on fire. Dashing this way and that, carrying this bundle and that suitcase, we dropped our threatened belongings, helter-skelter, in locations in the yard that later made no sense.

Many of our efforts were lifesaving. The boys wisely let all the fowl out of their pens—four or five skinny chickens, and one turkey we had kept because she had a chick, one I had been nursing, which I had shoved into the pocket of my shorts. They also set free several pigeons, hoping they would fly away into questionable freedom.

As the flames hissed and roared into our house, we all stood as far away from the crematorium as we could. Mom wet towels and clothing with muddy water and we draped them over our heads and shoulders. We stared at the burning house before us, our eyes streaming with tears, both from the pain in our hearts and from the stinging smoke. The sudden clicking sounds of Venetian blinds, as they caught fire and collapsed, sent shivers down our spines. Then, through the shooting flames came the most agonizing sound of all—the helpless groan of my piano as it thundered through the burning floor, resonating a chord so low, so discordant, and so haunting, it could only be interpreted as its death throes.

Our house went up like tinder, so rapidly that within a couple of hours all that was left were the heavy basement posts, transformed into incandescent pillars. The rest was one giant, smoldering ruin of ashes under a wild crisscrossing of iron bars from the windows and the twisted tin of our roof.

This many years later I remember watching the fire, staring into it as if I had been struck dumb. I had a wet towel slung across my shoulders. I held a hatbox filled with my belongings, and with my free hand I gripped my cousin Pat's tight little fingers. She was sobbing—a low, steady, tearless cry, like a child who has cried beyond tears after bitter punishment. In my pocket the baby turkey I had rescued stirred restlessly. If it made any sound, I did not hear it.

For many years, I had a recurring nightmare, where feelings of utter loss returned, and I experienced again the dawn of February 11. In the dream, I wandered with a group of refugees through a city of ashes, not knowing where to go or what to do.

My mother's face remains engraved in my memory. I can still envision her as she sat by the bonga, her face set as if in marble, her eyes fixed as if in death, her mouth a grim line, her shoulders hunched. Her face was turned away from the fiery remains of our house.

Beyond that, I don't recall much that happened in the remaining hours before daylight. I don't know whether I slept or sat up. I do recall the pain in my chest did not subside for days. I have a faint memory of lying on a mattress later in the day, watching embers flying like insects overhead, some of them landing on me, but not noticing any burns until much later when we would move into the shelter permanently, for what we knew would be a final fight for survival.

THE STEPS OF OUR BURNED-OUT HOME,
MARCH, 1945

XIV

February 11—We made camp. Brought all of our stuff as close to the shelter as we could, shoving it against the bamboo clump.

We only saved one bagful of rice and a cookie can full of sugar. For lunch we ate a few tablespoons of canned corned beef and a couple of teaspoons of peanut butter, which Aunt Rosemary surprised us with. We drank a few sips of water. We had saved a little powdered milk for the girls, which Patricia drank so fast she complained of a stomachache. Good thing she didn't drink the coconut milk I rescued—it was sour!

When the shooting and artillery barrage subsided, I crept toward the remains of our house. Each time I would look away from it, I expected to see the house intact, and was shocked to find a great pile of ashes and twisted bars and tin in its place. Remember it's gone, I told myself as I went back to the shelter after relieving myself in an area inside the clump of the bamboo we have cleared out. We dig holes as we need them and cover them up. Despite that, it still smells horrible in there.

We drooped around all day, spending hours inside the shelter, where we are so crowded we have to sleep propped up against one another. The boys can't stand it. They take refuge under the bamboo. Bert and Uncle Tito also have to get out and move around. They made sure our precious water filter is as close to the well as possible, but it's still about fifty feet from us.

That's too far away, considering how restricted our living area has become.

The street is deserted. We were surprised this evening when a man Bert knows shouted from the front gate. *"Good news! There are hundreds of American soldiers around Libertad Market. They'll be here very soon! Stay hidden. There is a big battle going on at the Rizal Stadium."*

He gave Bert a few more details, and Bert told him to give the Americans a message that they'd better speed it up and send some men to take care of the Japs holed up at the school. The man left, promising he would tell them. It was so hopeful to hear they are that close. No wonder there is so much firing around Vito Cruz. Rizal Stadium is just a few blocks away.

About an hour after this happened, we saw some people coming through the south side of the yard, where Uncle Tito and Bert pushed down the wire fence last night when they thought we might need an escape route. It was the Sabater family. They were struggling with a loaded pushcart, a couple of dogs trailing behind them. They dragged themselves into the yard and told us the most tragic story: Last night the Japs set all of Fresno Street on fire. As the Sabaters ran from the flames, a shell exploded and killed their youngest daughter. The mother, father, an older daughter and her husband, plus a couple of other relatives and their child, who looked to be about eight, were desperate to find shelter. Mrs. S. nursed the little finger of her left hand, which was hanging by a piece of skin. The little girl nursed a surface wound from shrapnel on her chest. Her poor father and the rest of them were all stained with blood; streaks of it had turned dark rust on their clothing and on their bare skin.

We set them up behind the shelter by the bamboo. At dusk we shared some rice and broth made from one of the chickens that was partly burned in the fire, its comb swollen to double its normal size. It was merciful to finally kill it. After dinner, the horrible events of the day caught up with Mrs. Sabater. She broke down. She could not stop sobbing. We worried the Japs would *hear her from the other side of the stone wall. Uncle Tito gave her sips of gin from a flask he had hidden under the camote vines that cover the top of the shelter.*

We spent the night in and out of the shelter, covering our ears to shut out the crack-crack *of rifle fire, machine gunning, and hollow* whoom-whoom *of mortar shells, all very close, coming from the street, the school, and from Vito Cruz.*

Heard terrible news from Mrs. Sabater's daughter, Mrs. Shultz. She told us Ulla's father was shot when he tried to stop the Japs from throwing petrol on the apartments. She said he has three bullet wounds in his chest, and the last she saw of him he was lying in an empty lot by his burned apartment, his family surrounding him. I can't imagine how Ulla must feel.

February 12, Monday—At the most, slept four hours last night. The shells and hand grenades, or mortars (it's sometimes hard to tell which) were falling like rain, for hours at a time. Through the shelter opening, where Mom sits praying the rosary, we felt the brunt of the concussion. The blasts bring in dirt and leaves. At one time it was extra violent, and we found out this morning the devastation was caused by a shell that blew apart the Camons' kitchen. Aunt Rosemary and I sneaked over to see the wreckage. We crouched on our knees to where the kitchen used to be. It doesn't exist. The entire house is a mess of shrapnel and wood splinters!

Since I was already out, I decided to grab a handful of rice crust from the bottom of the pot and take it to the fence between the Camons and us, where I left my canary, Pete, in his cage, hanging on a shrub, and the baby turkey lying in a cardboard box. I half-walked and half-crawled to the spot, and because the firing had not started up again, I stood up slowly to peer into the cage. Pete's little yellow body was lying stiff at the bottom of the cage. I never did get to look at the turkey, for just then a grenade or mortar—don't know which—blasted into the bonga palm. The concussion was brain-shattering. I was lifted and thrown to the ground. I had no sensation. I couldn't see. I couldn't hear, but I could still think, and I saw myself, whizzing down a dirt tunnel! All I could think of was, How come I'm dead and I can still think! A terrifying feeling—being dead but still trapped in consciousness—overwhelmed me. I was both frightened and angry. I traveled through the tunnel for a few seconds and then rose up miraculously to a line of light on a horizon, bright with sunlight. Adrenalin surged through me. I got up and raced to the shelter, screaming, "I'm hit! I'm hit!" Because my arms and neck felt numb, I was sure I had been hit.

Mom enveloped me in her arms and patted me all over saying, "You're O.K., Doreen. You're O.K.!"

The numbness disappeared after awhile. I was unhurt. I couldn't believe my luck. I think I could have used some of Uncle Tito's gin!

I spent rest of the morning in the shelter, with my head on my knees. All I could think is that we're now completely surrounded by danger. We are not safe anywhere. I doubt if we will see this through. Only yesterday when we heard the Yanks were in Libertad, we thought the worst was over.

I don't know what made me decide to crawl back to the ruins of the house that afternoon during another short lull. I think I must have been crazy after what I had experienced earlier. I simply felt compelled. After all this time, the ashes I crawled through were still warm. I felt I was visiting a grave, especially when I squatted down in the area where my room used to be. Absentmindedly, I ran my fingers through the ashes, which felt so fine, looked so purely gray, and smelled of dead fire. The ruins looked like scenes from a black and white movie—totally colorless. The street and the blocks and blocks of a burned-out landscape which surrounded us had no beginning and no end.

When my hand unexpectedly closed around a small hard object, I thought I had picked up a stone. Holding it up to the light, I gasped to see what I had found: It was the bisque figure of the infant Jesus from my nativity set! I could make out its tiny face and form, its features burned and blunted by the fire, with all but a few brushes of yellow paint remaining for straw, and traces of white paint for its gown. Spellbound, I stared at it. I could feel the warmth from its bier in the ashes, and as a glow passed through me, I, too, felt I had been warmed. Tears I had not shed since the fire fell onto my open palms and on the infant, making tiny dark splatters. When I closed my fist protectively around the Christ child, my tears spilled into the ashes, leaving little pits, like raindrops.

After a few moments, the firing began again and I made my way back to the shelter, fishtailing on my belly, and holding the baby Jesus in my clenched hand. "Mom, Mom!" I cried, look what I found!"

My mother was so stunned she pressed her fingers to her mouth and shook her head, "I can't believe it. It's a miracle!"

On and off all night, I pondered over the meaning of what I had experienced. Then in the dawn hours, surrounded by discord and pandemonium, it came to me. There was one chance in a million that I would find such a tiny object, with nothing else spared by the fire. One chance in a million, if that! And one chance in a million that it was not by chance, but rather a message from a power much greater than I? As I sorted through logical explanations, one clear truth remained—my sense of renewed hope. "We will survive," I said aloud. "We will survive!"

Then in the next hours, like the bullets speeding around us, new events started to pop. Uncle Tito and Bert, who had gone out to get some water from the filter, yelled at us from the south fence. "Come out! Come out!"

I was the last one to stumble out of the shelter. The sun blinded me. When I was able to focus, I couldn't believe what I saw. There, stood two American soldiers in khaki uniforms, wearing heavy helmets that were not like those worn before the war, their rifles pointing to the ground as they talked with Bert and Uncle Tito, wide grins spread on their perspiring faces. Mom and Aunt Rosemary ran up and hugged them. I could only stand and stare. Because of his blonde eyebrows, I guessed one of the men was fair; the other was dark-skinned and short. The blonde one drawled, "Wal, we came as fast as we could. Our outpost is five hundred yards south." He pointed a finger over his shoulder. His grin was so catching it made me break out in a laugh. "I think I'm going to have h-heart failure!" I stammered. I wanted that grin to remain on his face.

"Don't you have heart failure around me!" he exclaimed. Then he dropped his voice. "We're just scouts. Can't help you out of here. But we'll send help as soon as we get this area cleared. Stay in your shelter. You're in No-man's land."

They left as magically as they had arrived. The dark one turned back to me and with a puzzled look, asked, "How old are you?" He must have wondered who and what I was, seeing my grimy polka-dotted shorts, and mismatched red and white, stripped sailor blouse. Added to that I was barefoot, and totally filthy. My hair hung to my shoulders in matted strands.

"Seventeen," I answered. He mumbled something I couldn't catch, caught up with his partner and disappeared through the Camons' fence and onto Taft in the direction of Vito Cruz and the Rizal Stadium.

Their warning was valid. This afternoon the shooting got louder, if that is possible. The damned Japs (I can write what I feel now that the Yanks are here) tried to set fire to the school. Black smoke oozed upwards in columns, shooting up past the height of the bamboo. Periodically we heard them blasting, and we worried that the sheds would catch fire and torch our barricade of bamboo. Imagine—fifteen people dependent on the shelter and canopy of the bamboo. We made a kind of fort around the area, piling up all of our possessions. Eventually the school stopped smoking. About an hour after that, six American soldiers crawled by our south fence. Jim, who happened to be standing nearby, whistled to them. They paused, and listened in silence as we begged them to send some troops to the school to stop the Japs from doing anymore burning. They acted somewhat vague. They didn't seem to know anything about the streets around this area. Suddenly one of them looked toward Vito Cruz and said, "What's that?" Another yelled, "Heads up!" and they took off, crouched down low.

We heard a volley of gunfire around them as they vanished into the gray rubble of Taft Avenue toward Vito Cruz. Simultaneously, mortar fire exploded from the area of Menlo in back of the school. We ran for the shelter. Uncle Tito fell over Patricia and bumped into Don, who came limping into the shelter. It struck everyone as funny and we had to muffle our laughter.

We emerged a while later, to finish getting dinner of rice and broth again. It's so light it leaves us hungry. Our stomachs growl constantly. It's embarrassing. At the same time we moved some more of our stuff closer to the shelter. The minute we popped our heads out, zing, zing, zing, bullets ricocheted around us. Down on our stomachs; up for a second to move something; then down again. It got so intense that most of us had to remain in the shelter or stay squeezed up against the bamboo. Only the men stayed out to finish things up. Two more grenades or mortars fell, one on the Camons' garage, and the other near our mutual fence.

Bert, Uncle Tito, Don, Jim, and a couple of the Sabaters started back for the shelter when Uncle Tito turned back to pick up two bottles of water he had just filtered from the pump. We heard a third grenade or mortar go off. It landed squarely in our yard by the sound of it. Screams came from a smoke-filled area by the bonga. Bert yelled, "Dear, dear, Tito's hurt! Hurry!"

As we rushed out of the shelter, we saw Bert and Don partly carrying, partly dragging Uncle Tito. He was a mass of dripping blood—it was gushing from his legs and from one arm. They set him down at the mouth of the shelter in the open trench, and Mom started first aid on him. I marveled at how cool she seemed as she applied a tourniquet on an artery wound on his left leg, close to his ankle. She instructed Aunt Rosemary to hold up his leg while she worked. My aunt was shaking so badly Mom had to

yell at her. Bert held up Uncle's right leg, which was also bleed-
ing badly but not from an artery.

Uncle Tito turned a greenish white and began to faint. He
moaned, "I'm hit. I'm no use. Go in the shelter and protect your-
selves." He reached for Patricia, who knelt by his head, crying
hysterically. He asked her and Posy to kiss him.

"My Daddy is dying," Patricia repeated over and over. Posy
whimpered and squeezed her little hands together. I put my arms
around them both and told them to come into the shelter with
me—that the best way to help their Daddy was to stop crying and
take cover. At first, Patricia refused. "I want to stay with my
Daddy."

Gently I pulled her away from her father, who lay like death,
with his eyes closed, and his mouth suddenly slack. "Auntie Ma-
ria, Mommy, and Uncle Bert will take care of him. He won't
die!" I cried, hoping to convince myself as well.

As I herded my cousins into the shelter, I turned to see Mrs.
Shultz sitting, looking lifeless, by the bonga, her face covered
with rivulets of blood, and her parents laying cloths on her head
to try to stop the bleeding. Later we found out a bullet had
lodged at the base of her skull. She is partly paralyzed.

Mom was able to stop the blood from gushing from my un-
cle's artery. Apparently, a bullet tore into it. The rest of his
wounds are from shrapnel. Thank God he smokes and has a hab-
it of throwing his silver cigarette case down his shirtfront. The
case was badly dented and twisted by shrapnel.

Mom and Aunt Rosemary forced a small mattress into the
trench for him. They made a barricade around him from pillows
and pieces of tin from the roof of the house. It was quickly get-
ting dark. After Uncle Tito was settled on the mattress, the color
coming back into his face, we stopped to eat a ration of raw
corned beef and drank some water. Salt from the beef, coupled
with the brackish taste of water made me feel like throwing up.

Patricia and Posy calmed down and fell right to sleep on the
floor of the shelter. The mosquitoes were driving me crazy. Luck-

ily, I found a fragment of old mosquito netting in a pile of bedding and tied a couple of ends to the shelter posts. What a set-up, but at least it helped to keep some of the insects from chewing us up. My brothers and Bert slept on the ground by the bamboo. Mom and Aunt Rosemary took turns watching over Uncle Tito, so Pat and Posy and I had a little more room in the shelter and were able to sleep, despite the mosquitoes buzzing, and dirt from the sides of the shelter falling on us each time a big blast hit. We slept for several hours able to ignore the eruption of rifles, machine guns, grenades and mortars exploding around us all night long.

February 13—The Camons' bedroom received a direct hit. It looks as bad as their bathroom, but not as bad as their kitchen. They've retreated to their shelter. Mrs. Shultz was delirious all night long. Miraculously, Uncle Tito is better today. We can't imagine how he survived the grenade or mortar that landed five or six yards from him. We moved his mattress into the shelter. He has the entire front wing. It has to be that way because it's an impossibility to stay outside even a few feet without cover.

I can't exactly describe our situation in words, as I would like to. I believe that no one, no matter how much they read about war or hear about it, can imagine one-tenth of what it is to be in the middle of a battle. We don't even know whether Japs or Americans sneak through our yard at night, but we see their shadows and hold our breaths. Maxie and Skippy are so shell-shocked they don't bark, but shiver and shake, and stay as close to us as they can.

Mr. Sabater foolishly sneaked back to his gutted house before lunch. He was met by six Japs, who, by the luck of his life, only pushed him around and searched him! He brought back the news that many known families in this area were burned to death or hacked to pieces by the Japs. He told us that a Mr. Stam (?), a Swiss, was bayoneted. Bert felt badly. He knew him.

We are sure Japs are hidden at the school who watch our every move. When he peeked over the stone fence, Jim spotted

*one firing a knee mortar. If the Americans weren't so close, they
would come and finish us off. Actually, they are trying to pick us
off; otherwise, it wouldn't make sense that so many bullets, grenades, and mortars land in our yard. The shells that have hit the
Camons and our old garage are obviously from farther away.*

*The activity around us was further explained by something
that happened yesterday, which I forgot to mention. After we saw
our first American, a guerrillero came through our yard. He had
been nicked in the head by a sniper bullet. He informed us this
district is full of Jap snipers hiding all around us in trees, under
the shambles of burned houses, in empty shelters—everywhere.
He said he believes that the Mitsui has some as well. Thank God
our gate was locked on the night of the fire, and continues to be.*

*At lunch Mom sneaked out to fix a quick lunch at the far end
of the shelter. We have difficulty moving around we are so
cramped. We can hardly go out for water. Jim had just taken an
empty pail to fill it with water when he was shot at. He threw
himself on the ground. Moments later he returned for the pail
and found it riddled with holes. Everything we own has been
touched by gunfire. The few pieces of furniture we left in the
front yard are full of holes. Our narra dining room table is only
good for firewood. A huge shell crater blasted through its fine
satin top.*

*The last of our chickens was wandering around the yard and
was hit by shrapnel. It was terrible to see it jumping around with
its head half off! We made broth with it for dinner, and everything went well until I passed a bowl of the soup to Uncle Tito
lying on his mattress. He was passing me a glass of water at the
same time. When I said, "Here," he thought that I was reaching
for the glass, when, actually, I was passing the soup to him! The
soup and the glass collided and fell all over him, Patricia, and
the shelter floor. I started to giggle, and soon Patricia was
screaming with laughter. Needless to say, Uncle Tito didn't think
it was so funny. We didn't laugh long. Everyone hushed us up.
We are nine sleeping in the shelter tonight. Some of us are sitting
up, others are curled up and bumping into one another's heads,*

arms, and legs. Don ended up sleeping at the shelter entrance next to Bert. Mom dozed a little and then sat up to guard, and pray her rosary. I felt like a bunch of broken bones, but I finally fell asleep.

February 14, Wednesday—Woke up with a start. Three grenades had just burst near our shelter. Mrs. Shultz, who was lying by the bamboo, got some shrapnel in her mattress. We all jumped up when the rat-tat-tat *from machine guns blasted only a few feet away. More hand grenades added to the chaos. We had practically no breakfast. I feel sick. The girls do nothing but cry they are hungry. It's our end. We have no chance. One of those shells is bound to hit the shelter sooner or later.*

There were lulls during the day of five to ten minutes. During one of these respites I crawled into the bamboo to relieve myself. Some of the branches have been torn off by gunfire in that part of the stand. I can't help who saw me. At least no bullets followed me!

Toward lunchtime firing came to a stop. The Camons started yelling to us that the Americans are now in the school! Thank God. Two soldiers waved to them over the stone wall. They called us all over, and one of them said, "It's a damned good thing you didn't stir last night. We'd have killed you, thinking you were Japs!" They also said they lost twenty-two men out of a unit of thirty who had taken over the school. Jap snipers had attacked them with rifles and mortars. They don't call them grenades. I guess we've been having mostly mortars land all around us. They found one of the snipers in the sheds. He was probably shooting at us!

The soldiers warned us to get out of here as fast as we can. We're in the middle of the front lines. There is a huge battle going on at the Rizal Stadium. They can't believe we're still alive. They looked down in the dumps and acted jittery, telling us they can't leave their post to help us. But they assured us there's an outpost a block or two South, on Taft, in an empty lot. They think they can send medics if we can let them know where we are.

Bert is very brave. Unarmed, he took the risk of crawling through the firing and rubble to the outpost. Amazingly, he returned unharmed, escorted by eight soldiers bearing a couple of stretchers for Uncle Tito and Mrs. Shultz. Poor Mrs. Shultz cried when they placed her on a stretcher. The soldiers told us we couldn't take much, so we took a few cans of precious corned beef and some clothes. We divided all the items among us. We were instructed to sneak forward at least six to twelve paces apart. A soldier guarded us as we ran forward. I headed up the first group with Aunt Rosemary, the girls, and Uncle Tito on a stretcher borne by two medics. "Go, go, go!" the soldiers ordered, and I ran for my life. I don't even recall how I ended up in a foxhole surrounded by three bearded American soldiers!

The outpost was an open field with a few foxholes filled with dirty, tired infantrymen who stared at us as if we had dropped out of the sky. Soon they were laughing. One of them said, "We didn't know they had hillbillies in the Philippines!"

I felt like a dwarf standing up in a foxhole with three huge soldiers. They kept shaking their heads in disbelief, but by their eyes I knew they were as happy to see me, as I was to be with them. "Happy Valentine's Day," a black-bearded one smiled. My heart leaped!

Shortly afterwards we were led from the fighting lines by several soldiers to Taft and down towards Pasay, to the home of a Swiss family, the Bosshards. (Not sure how they spell their name).

Here we are now as refugees. All I can say is "Thank you, Jesus!"

XV

February 15, Thursday—Woke up this morning aching like the very devil, but thank God we slept. I kept rolling off my mattress, which was on the floor of Mrs. B's bedroom. I kept dreaming of the explosions and woke up several times with a start. In my dreams I was hit. Mom, who shared Mrs. B's bed, had nightmares also, and talked in her sleep. She kept repeating, "Get down! Get down! I'm awake, I'm awake!"

Never mind. It's heaven to sleep stretched out on a mattress and to feel safer. The Americans have gun emplacements in a second outpost less than a block away. Their shelling shakes the ground, but we have the satisfaction they are giving the Japs at the Stadium HELL.

We are close to Libertad Market. This morning some women from this neighborhood planned to see if the market was open. They were led back by GIs because a dozen Jap snipers were picking people off. Later, our soldiers and four tanks went up that way to take care of them.

Just around the corner the GIs killed another sniper. Bert and the boys went to see him. When they came back they said that half his head was blown off. The Filipinos who pass him throw rocks and spit on the corpse.

This morning we heard from the GIs that it's not safe to go back to our yard, but this afternoon they said it was fairly safe to return to pick up our remaining food and clothing, valuables we can't afford to let the looters, who are stealing everywhere, take.

Bert sneaked back and returned with most of our things, including poor Maxie, who had to be left behind because the soldiers told us we couldn't take our animals. Somehow Mom managed to hide Skippy under some clothing when she crossed the lines. Poor Maxie had some shrapnel wounds on his back. He was so glad to see us he couldn't stop yipping! Good thing Bert hurried back, for Mr. Camon, who followed him with a pushcart, was just missed by a grenade.

Mrs. Shultz was taken to the Chinese hospital we were told by her parents, who also got out of our yard yesterday. Uncle Tito is much better, but he'll also be going to a hospital to be checked.

This afternoon we watched an impressive line of tanks pass by. We waved and made the V sign. One soldier threw a half eaten candy bar at me, and I reached for it as if it were a bride's bouquet. We met Colonel Soriano, a prominent Manila businessman, who left with the Bataan generals and who had been reported killed. He eyed us, came closer and said, "Don't you know me? I'm Soriano."

Mom and Bert finally recognized him and they shook hands. The Colonel knows Grandma well and asked about her. When Mom told him she was at Uncle Pepe's house by the Rizal Stadium, he looked serious and didn't say anything. We are really worried about them. Someone else who got out of the Vito Cruz area says La Salle College has been practically razed to the ground. The Japs killed a lot of civilians taking shelter in the chapel. Even the priests were murdered! We heard more horror stories about hundreds of civilians being shot or burned to death. The prominent Perez-Rubio family, who lives right on Vito Cruz, was all killed.

February 16—Who should come over this morning but Porky and his friend Pocholo. It was so good to see them. I got a lump in my throat. Everyone in the apartments was liberated last Sunday by three American soldiers. Porky said they sent someone to come and tell us, but we never heard about it. Pocholo is very sad because he lost some aunts and uncles who live by Vito

Cruz. There was a terrible fight there— worse than it was for us. We're so worried about Grandma and the family. We felt some relief when we heard that someone saw a lot of people in that area were still alive and were picked up and taken by trucks to relief camps in Santa Anna yesterday afternoon and this morning. More good news—Rizal Stadium is taken! It's relatively safe now, up to San Andrés Street.

The Philippine General Hospital was also taken today. Every patient, doctor, and nurse died—all of them slaughtered by the Japs. No one dares think what has happened in the Ermita, where fighting is still going on. We also heard that the Walled City is now another bloody battleground. The Japs are holed inside buildings in a desperate last-ditch-stand. Our troops are fighting, block by block.

The soldiers from the outpost—a weapons troop from the First Cavalry—are so thoughtful. They gave us peas, corn, Spam, bread and coffee. What a feast! We all stood around their jeeps and foxholes while we ate. They also gave some food to hungry Filipinos. We are getting to know several of the men from the troop. They are Frank Kayatta, John Smedley, John Kuhlman, Max (somebody), and about ten others whose names I don't remember.

We were still eating when a warning came from the field that there was a sniper in the immediate area. The GIs were ready in less than two minutes: the machine gunners were at their guns; the rifle men packed their rifles and started moving up the road and into the field. Don, Jim, and I were quickly led into a foxhole, which was next to Frank's, who sat manning a machine gun. The soldiers ordered us to crouch down. I got hold of a helmet and put it on. Frank turned around as calm as anything, grinned, and said, "You've got it on backward, but you look cute."

Some of the boys came back for hand grenades and went up the road. Soon we heard bullets whiz. They returned in a few minutes, laughing and remarking on the "big catch." They killed the sniper up the road. He was hiding in a nipa shack that was

*all nailed up. John Smedley was the one who killed him; the rest
of the boys riddled the corpse to bits. I've got a button and an
autograph from Smedley. The rest of them thought it amusing;
they had never heard of anyone wanting a button as a souvenir.*

*When we returned to the house we heard more bad news
brought in by people who drop by and tell us what is happening.
Countless families have been slaughtered in all parts of Manila.
We hear bits and pieces of information, some of it positive, such
as the news that, after the Tabacalera was burned to the ground,
the Japs let the people evacuate the area and cross the Pasig.
We hope Uncle Ovidio, Auntie Teresita, Aunt Blanca and the
kids were among them.*

*February 17, Saturday—Mr. Bosshard went to Santo Tomás.
When he returned he had a note from my father. He is all right
and was desperate to hear news of us. He had seen Grandma,
Uncle Pepe and family, Auntie Teresita and Uncle Ovidio, who
have all survived! Grandma was taken to the hospital. During
the fighting, she panicked and ran off into a field near their shelter. She was rescued by several GIs and treated for shock and
dehydration. According to Mr. B., my dad is skin and bones. He
didn't see Aunt Lolita, Aunt Blanca, or Aunt Annie, but all survived.*

*No civilians are yet allowed in Santo Tomás. Mr. B. got in by
chance. It's almost impossible to get across craters, hanging
wire, destroyed pillboxes and dead Japs along the way. The internees look pretty bad. They have suffered starvation, many
since September. Some of the buildings in the camp are dam-
aged, but, all in all, that area suffered the least in Manila because the Americans got to it sooner.*

*I am so relieved everyone in the family is safe. The soldiers
who were here when we got the news were very glad for us. You
could see it in their eyes. We all feasted for dinner. Mr. B.
brought butter, cheese, bread, and surprised us with some of the
latest magazines from the Army. It was such a thrill to see an
honest to goodness up-to-date magazine!*

February 18, Sunday—The boys at the corner did a lot of shooting last night. Their trap flare went off. We found out this morning that they didn't catch any snipers. A dog had set the flare off. I didn't go down until later. I had to catch up with my diary. Russell, one of the soldiers from the weapon's troop, joined me on the porch. He had some letter writing to do. He told me their unit expects to leave this outpost.

This afternoon I had my picture sketched by an artist from their group. Frank asked him to do it. The rest of the guys teased him. They say he has a crush on me! Anyway, I was glad to do it. Frank looked so pleased. The artist also sketched Patricia, who has made a hit with all the boys. While the artist was working, smiling GIs from the troop surrounded me. I signed my portrait: "To Frank—one of the swell guys who liberated Manila."

More activity later this afternoon when a jeep drove up with some Swiss kids, who gave us more bad news. Forty Swiss are missing, among them Liselotte and her folks. Ole Hansen, a classmate, lost his brother Nels. A shell exploded in his face in the Ermita, which remains a bloody battleground. The main fighting is concentrated in the Walled City now.

February 19—Today we went down to the outpost to say good-bye to the boys. The poor fellows looked so blue. When it came time to shake hands, they looked the other way. We wished them all the luck in the world. Johnny K. looked as if he was going to cry. I felt like crying myself, and I would have if the ordeal had lasted much longer.

We must make plans to move on. The B's have hosted us long enough. We would like to go to Santo Tomás, which is becoming a repatriation camp. Bert left early this morning to see if they could take us in, but he was turned away because too many homeless civilians have scaled over the walls. In the meantime, the internees are being prepared for evacuation to the States.

Bert reported that he couldn't recognize a lot of old friends in camp because they are so thin and emaciated. He said he was told that, had the Americans not rescued them when they did, they would all have been killed. Apparently the attack wasn't scheduled until March, but a Japanese civilian in Santo Tomás by the name of Tobo send a secret message to MacArthur, telling him to hurry up and liberate the camp before the internees were massacred.

We heard more details about the fighting in the Walled City, where men, women, and children were lined up and bayoneted. Hundreds of girls and women there, and throughout Manila, were raped and killed. The Japs threw babies in the air and bayoneted them. There are very few districts that were spared Japanese brutality. The count keeps going up. We won't know how many died until it's over. The shelling and fighting in the Walled City is so intense we hope it will end soon. When it does, it will mean that most of Manila will be liberated.

We thought the Weapons Troop was going to the Walled City, but heard that after they leave La Salle, they will go to the Luneta, which is close to the Walled City.

February 20—False alarm. Early today, we were told we could move to Santo Tomás, so we packed up early and were able to get transportation via an Army ambulance. But once we arrived in camp, we were turned away. The Army issued an order, stating that until Santo Tomás is cleared of people who have not been formally checked in, no one else can be accepted. There is no more room.

The trip to and from the camp is one I will never forget. We drove down Dominga Street, out Santa Scholastica, and onto Paco. From there, we made more than ten detours. If I live to be sixty, I'll never forget the ride. We went through miles and miles of dusty road, not recognizing any landmarks. On both sides of the streets houses are razed to the ground—ruin, ruin, ruin. The stench is sickening—dead people everywhere, bloated and burned. Refugees stand around on street corners, their eyes blank.

MPs kept stopping us. They wouldn't let us over one of the pontoon bridges to cross the Pasig, but we detoured, and guided by a jeep, we got over the former Jones Bridge.

When we finally got to the camp, we were hemmed in by hundreds of other people trying to get in. We had stood more than an hour when Bert spotted my father, Uncle Tommy, Aunt Lolita, Carol, and Auntie Teresita and Uncle Ovidio. They talked to a guard, assuring him we were only visitors, and he allowed us in.

I didn't expect to choke up, but I couldn't help it when I saw Dad and the rest of them. Dad came up to me and said, "Hello, honey," and kissed my cheek.

It's been three years! I hardly recognized him. He is so, so thin! His cheeks looked all sucked in and his skinny arms dangled. But his blue eyes sparkled and he looked so glad to see me. Don and Jim are about as tall as he is, which surprised him. We are all thin, but nothing like those who starved. Uncle Tommy laughed and told us he has already gained fifteen pounds.

I asked Dad about Grannie and Grandad. They had left Remedios Hospital several months before the fighting and were back in camp. Grandad was ailing badly from heart problems. He and Dad had never been close, but when my father told me my grandfather had died the day after the camp was liberated, his eyes watered, and I heard his throat close up for several moments. He said Grannie was all right, but didn't get around too well because she is quite weak from the effects of malnutrition.

After we visited with the family, I wandered around looking for Marcia but never found her. I did see others I knew, including the Brooks twins. I shook hands with them, and then I noticed there was another young boy with them, whom I didn't recognize. When he came up and said, "Hello, Doreen!" I knew his voice. Paul Davis, another of my eighth grade classmates! Before the war he was the picture of health. He is very thin and gaunt now, and his eyes are so sad. No wonder—he lost his father, and his sister Ann bled to death when she was hit by a shell after they were liberated! I couldn't believe it. Ann, I knew her so well. She was always such fun. It doesn't seem real. There were fifteen internees killed in the shelling and ninety wounded.

*The poor Brooks twins have suffered a terrible loss also: Their
parents both died of starvation.*

*The sight of my emaciated classmates with their devastating
news gave me a deep, sick feeling in my stomach. We left the
camp after visiting with friends and family for three hours. I was
glad to get out of the hot sun and anxious to have something to
eat, having had nothing since breakfast.*

*We were cheered on the way back to see Liselotte and her
family trudging around the Paco ruins with a loaded pushcart.
They were just getting out of Isaac Peral in the Ermita. Apparently they had just been liberated. They all looked like we must
have on the fourteenth—filthy and exhausted. We couldn't stop
the truck, but waved madly to them.*

*Along the way, Mr. Camon, who rode with us, yelled to a
friend riding by on a bike. "Hello, where are you going?"*

The friend answered. "Home."

Mr. C. yelled back. "You still got a home to go to?"

*That's everyone's story. Lucky those, who still have a home
to go to.*

*Accounts of atrocities continue coming in from liberated ar-
eas of the city. We heard that Mrs. Klein and Mrs. Lyttle (not
sure how to spell their names), friends of Mom and Bert's, were
picked up by the Japs somewhere in the Ermita. They were taken
to the Bay View Hotel where they were raped and killed.*

*When we visited Auntie Teresita at Santo Tomás, she said
they had not saved a thing when the J's burned the Tabacalera.
Along with others from the factory, they took refuge in a nearby
convent. They had to walk over dead and wounded lying in the
streets. The Japs shelled and threw grenades into the convent.
Half of the refugees perished. Those who were left, among them
Auntie, Uncle, Aunt Blanca and the kids, crossed the Pasig into
American-held territory. Auntie also told us that Grandma, Aunt
Annie, cousin Johnny, Uncle Pepe, Aunt Carmen and the chil-
dren were all going to a house in Santa Anna. We hadn't heard
earlier that Uncle Pepe had suffered a shrapnel wound on his*

back and had had to spend a couple of days in the hospital. He is O.K. and is back with the family. I can hardly keep up with all the news about our relatives, but feel very relieved that almost everyone survived. I was sorry about Grandad, and sick that so many died in camp. I feel so saturated with news of death and suffering I can't bear to hear of another tragedy, yet I must know what has happened to everyone.

February 21, Wednesday—It's one week ago today that we came out of Hell. One week of American liberation—a wonderful, incredible week! We are free, really free, and we can call our souls our own at last.

The situation improves by the day. Things are becoming more and more normal. I can't get used to seeing our old coins back, jingling in our pockets! We can buy things for practically nothing. And thank God, we have our lives, our health, and enough food to eat.

There are several main points of fighting in Manila—the Walled City, the Post Office Building, the Port Area, and University of the Philippines. There is still Japanese infiltration in other sections, but all in all, the situation is improving. You know, almost every soldier we've talked to thought Manila wouldn't be a battleground.

Frank K. came to see us this afternoon. He had just killed a sniper by La Salle College. He was awfully sweaty and acted very shy. Smedley came awhile later. He says it's still tough by the college—bullets everywhere. Two of the boys from the outfit were blown up by a land mine this morning. I didn't ask who they were, because I don't think I could bear to hear about any more killings.

The only good news we heard this afternoon is that Cabanatuan and Bilibid POWs were let free. According to the GI who gave us the news, there were over five hundred prisoners liberated from Cabanatuan. I pray Harry may be among them, but I am not hopeful.

February 22—It's Washington's Birthday and I can mention it without fearing censorship. I've had to keep it quiet for three years, and I still can't get used to the freedom of saying and writing what I think.

Don Kiefer, one of Mrs. Bosshard's relatives, came out of camp to see her. He told us that the Mencarinis were beheaded by the Japs, and that their three kids are now in camp. I remember their daughter Elvira well, and I can't imagine how she must feel. Mr. Kiefer also gave us news that three-hundred-and-sixty American internees had left on a transport plane. Marcia and her family were among them! Darn! I wanted to see her so badly! The Wilsons, good friends of our family, were also on board. I hope they have a good trip and can settle in the States. How wonderful for them. It's our hope to eventually be repatriated also. Right now, though, I have a need to stay in Manila, to see an end to the fighting, and, perhaps, to see the city begin to rise out of the ashes.

February 23—We got some cloth rationed by the Red Cross. They gave us eight meters of cheap blue check. We traded some of our cloth with Mrs. Camons' polka dotted fabric, and Mrs. Bosshard sold us some of hers. It was great to be able to cut out some blouses and begin sewing them up.

Later I had to brace myself when I heard of more killings. A friend of Mrs. B's spent nine days without water or food, together with hundreds of others who were hiding in the Elena Apartments. The Japs locked them up there and murdered them after they had raped the women, some of them girls of ten and twelve. Mrs. Bosshard was so upset by the news she left the room and cried out that she didn't want to hear any more about it.

This afternoon brought news of more atrocities. Mr. Kiefer, Pedro Picornell, and some GIs stopped over. I know Pedro and his family. When I asked him how everyone was, he told us the most upsetting story. During the crisis he was in the Remedios Hospital helping to care for the wounded. He actually saw Nels Hansen, and his own brother, Jimmy, when they we were hit by a shell, which exploded while they were carrying a stretcher. Ped-

*ro was carrying an end of the same stretcher and he only suf-
fered a scratch on his leg. For fifteen days they ate only teaspoons of condensed milk. One night Pedro says he counted fifteen hundred shells falling around them. No one knows why the
hospital was a target. He saw his brother suffer for five hours,
minus an arm and a leg before he died. My God!*

*Pedro has joined the Army for revenge. He is one brave guy.
Before he left he also mentioned some other deaths. Angelita
Perez and Roberto Soloaga were killed by the Japs. Hearing
about all the killings left me feeling exhausted, as if I couldn't
take a full breath.*

*I guess this has been a bad day altogether, for when Bert re-
turned from a trip to his old office, he reported the bodega where
he had hidden one-half of my diary, with entries from 1942-
1943, was burned. Not a trace of it left.*

*We had a family conference this evening, and decided we are
going back to our old place to share the Camons' house until we
have more definite news of what is to become of us. There is a
PCAU (Philippine Civil Affairs Unit) relief station at the old
school, which will be a godsend, as Bert has less than one hundred pesos left.*

*February 26—Today we started moving back to the Camons.
Bert, the boys, and Mr. C. made many trips with the pushcarts
loaded. Mrs. Bosshard lent us some furniture—four chairs, two
settees, a table and a couch. We'll be in style once we get everything cleaned up there.*

*Left right after lunch and started cleaning up the house as
soon as we arrived. It was no easy task to sweep up all the
shrapnel, wood splinters, and glass lying all over the place. But
by dinnertime we had things looking fairly picked up. It was a
treat to sit down after we ate in a quiet, candlelit sala. It was
almost homey. It beats the racket we had at the Bosshard's.
There were just too many of us.*

*Mrs. Camon told us our fortunes before we went to bed. We
turned in early. I slept like a log despite a worry that snipers
might get in through the shelled-out kitchen! It's still not totally*

safe. The boys went out to the yard, and when they turned on a flashlight—bang! Someone shot at them. Bert said it was proba-bly an American bullet. No end to the irony.

February 27—Started out by sweeping and bunuting the floor. The coconut husk kept slipping from under my foot, but I was able to bring quite a shine to the floor. Mr. C. was upset because he saw some of his furniture in nipa shacks near by. The looters even took the toilet fixtures.

Later had a treat when three fellows we have met offered to give us a ride around the city. We got into their jeep and swung around the Wak Wak and San Juan areas. It's so lovely on the other side of the river. Everything is so peaceful, and there are camps and camps of U.S. soldiers in the fields of Quezon City. Reconstruction is already beginning. We passed bridges and saw downed wires being fixed.

We ended up at Santo Tomás, where Mr. Carrol, Bert's for-mer boss, let us in past the lines of waiting refugees. I saw sev-eral of my schoolmates. One of them, Jeanette West, who was a year ahead of me, took me around the shantytowns, where in-ternees rigged up little nipa shacks. Jeanette was looking for the names of a hundred girls from camp to attend a dance for enlist-ed men at Grace Park on Friday. I sure wish my name could have been included.

I saw my friend Bill Hoffman as he drove by with some other schoolmates. I waved to him and I think he recognized me. I wouldn't have known him if Jeanette hadn't pointed him out. Like everyone else, he is a shadow of his former self.

Just before we left, I ran into General Casey, our old neigh-bor from Protacio Street. He was a Captain when I saw him last. He is a Brigadier General now! He shook hands with us and told us that Hugh Boyd, now nineteen, is a Second Lieutenant and is due to come into camp in a few days. Imagine! He also said Keith and the family are doing fine. Bert asked him if it is possi-ble for us to get some rations. The general talked to someone in the administration office and told us they would try to make ar-rangements.

February 29—Today ends another month. It has been the most glorious and the most tragic month in my life, likewise, in the history of the Philippines. Manila is nothing but ashes, but we have been liberated. I became so emotional this evening I wrote another poem—a twin to the one I wrote as infamous February began.

A LONG NIGHT ENDED

Three years we were under them,
Three years—just one long night,
A night just ended,
In a bloody, terrible fight.

Manila has been redeemed.
The Japs are six feet under,
But miles and miles of desolation and death
Are signs of their horrible plunder.

They burned the city and shelled the rest.
Civilians they picked off like flies.
Their Co-prosperity Sphere and magnanimity
Were a pack of damnable lies.

The fight is over, Manila is free,
And a few have lived to tell
The tale of three years of Japanese rule
That all of us know too well.

But now, we're free, the Yanks have come,
It's the end of that long night.
Providence helped us; the wrong has failed,
And God has defended the right.

March 1, Thursday—Mom and Bert left early this morning for Saint Joseph's Hospital to visit Grandma, who is suffering from severe anemia. She is due for a blood transfusion. She is excited she will be getting an American soldier's blood!

We had a busy day. Don went to the PCAU but came back with only rice. By incredible coincidence we had a visit from an old friend, Paul Kundirk, who gave us the case of corned beef that saved our lives. He surprised us, his arms loaded with canned goods and more fabric! He is still in the Army and said he is glad he can help. I'm grateful we could thank him again for what he did for us.

Mom and Bert returned from their visit to see Grandma. She is well taken care of. In fact, they met a Chaplain and his aide, a corporal by the name of Glenn Pinnell. The Chaplain and Glenn had been visiting with her. We also had a good visit with them when they drove by later on.

Bad news about PCAU at the school: They are moving to another part of the city. The school will become a hospital. Never mind, their rations were really not adequate. Change is happening all around. The PCAU was only at the school for a few days!

Trouble here as well. Mr. Camon and three soldier friends got hold of some Scotch and got tipsy. Mr. C. was rude to Mom at dinner. Bert was furious with him and later told us that it will be time to move again soon. I hope we can get into Santo Tomás.

One reason the soldiers had booze is that the fighting is getting over with and they are in rest camp at Wak Wak. You can't blame them.

March 6—Was deathly sick today with fits of vomiting and diarrhea. Half the city is suffering from the same upset. They blame the water, which is still not totally purified. I am also sensitive to smell. In the last few days, hundreds of Jap corpses in the boulevard area are being cremated. The stench is horrible—enough to make anyone throw up.

I was treated at the new hospital at the school for some ringworm spreading on the back of my thigh. I've never had anything like it before. I know it comes from filth. What a mess! The day would have ended terribly had it not been for the fact that Bert was informed by the administration at Santo Tomás that it looks like we may soon be able to get in. He has been offered a job in the office!

March 7, Wednesday—One day was all it took. We are in Santo Tomás! To make a long story short, we were given permission to enter by Colonel Gregorie himself. Bert was given a job in the office as comptroller. We arrived at 5 P.M. in a U.S. Army truck and were taken to a shanty right next door to Uncle Tommy's, where we were all fixed up in no time as we had very little moving to do. It's wonderful here with all the kids, the GIs, and the food.

Tonight there was a dance in the big plaza out in front of the main building. I stayed in bed all morning, still sick, but I went to the dance with my old friend Georgie. I had to leave early because the nausea caught up with me.

THE SHAMBLES THAT WAS MANILA,
12 FEBRUARY 1945

U.S. Navy Photo 114-10

XVI

The move to Santo Tomás was the beginning of our adjustment to a new life. The occupation was behind us. We had survived the fire and the battle. We were still staggering from the horror of the holocaust, but were beginning to heal, little by little, day by day. Each day reassured us of our freedom. There was sunshine, there was food, there was music—we even saw Irving Berlin—and we were all together in our nipa shacks. For me personally, the dazzle of activities in the camp captivated me. I met old friends. We went to dances, movies, and meet handsome young soldiers. We gossiped and laughed and enjoyed typical teen-age friendships. I began to wear lipstick. I had some new clothes, blouses Mom and I had sewn, plus a new yellow dress made by a camp seamstress. It had a circular skirt and I loved tripping around in it.

I wrote less devotedly in my diary. There was too much else to occupy my time. Writing had been a lifeline for me, but I depended on it less after liberation. I met a reporter from the First Cavalry, Pete Olwyler, who read my poems and some of my diary entries. He encouraged me to keep on writing. He was bright, intuitive, good-looking, and he loved to dance as much as I did. I fell for him hard. After he left the camp for the mountains, where the Japs were still holed in, I suffered from a broken heart. At the same time I found myself absorbed in goings-on in camp.

I did not forget Harry. The Red Cross was able to give me his parents' address in Grand Junction, Colorado. I wrote to them and received a heartfelt letter from his mother. She had not heard from him for over a year and had only received a couple of short notes sent through the Red Cross. She thanked us for keeping in touch with Harry and mentioned that she had had dreams about a family who was helping her son. I answered her letter immediately and promised I would keep in touch with her.

It was not until months later when we were in Richmond, California, that we received a grief-stricken letter informing us that Harry was missing and was presumed dead. He was one of eighteen hundred POWs shipped from the Philippines on an unmarked Japanese transport, the *Arisan Maru*, which was torpedoed by an American sub two hundred miles north of Luzon on the South China Sea. The ship was on its way to Japan loaded with POWs, who were locked up in the holds. Only eight men survived. The ship went down on October 24, 1944—the day I wrote I had had a vision of Harry lying in a wheat field. I had hoped with all my heart that he had survived, although I had a strong feeling that he had not. Thoughts of him still light my life. He has lived as a symbol of endurance and bravery.

As we prepared for repatriation to the United States in late April, after almost everyone else had left the camp, I still had mixed feelings about leaving Manila. I wanted to stay to witness the city grow back into what it had been before the war. At the same time, I yearned for a new life in the U.S., a boundless country, full of opportunity.

The closeness Mom, Bert, Don, Jim and I had experienced during three years of occupation was replaced by a sense of watchful independence. We kept an eye on one another, but needed to be on our own as well. We knew the bond we had shared would always be there.

Almost ten years had passed since we experienced our first Christmas on Peñafrancia Street—The Christmas of one hundred candles—a decade that was so packed with experience it equaled several life times. I looked forward to the tenth Christmas in the States. I thought about that as I packed my things to get ready to board the *Monterey*, a troopship that was to take us from Manila

Bay on May 7. As I wrapped the charred image of the baby Jesus in tissue paper and placed it carefully in my suitcase, I marveled at how important the nativity set had been during the three Christmases of occupation. For a moment, scenes of the fire flashed in my mind, bringing back the loss. Finding the infant in the ashes had been a miracle of renewed hope. I vowed that someday I would put the faded little figure in a manger, in celebration of some far-off Christmas in a new land.

May 7—As 9:15 A.M. approached, I got more and more nervous. Finally the hour arrived and the announcement came over the camp radio for us to take our luggage to the plaza, where the trucks were waiting to take us to the pier. Our friends were all there to say good-bye. One of them ran to the radio room and played I'm Just Wild About Harry. *That got to me! Tears streamed down my cheeks. All of us cried.*

We piled into the trucks quickly and were soon down the drive. I could still see everyone waving by the main building. The fire trees were in bloom, their red blossoms bright in the morning sun. When we got to the piers, I was shocked to see piles of wreckage strewn around the docks, including some unexploded shells.

A "Duck," an Army amphibian, took us out to the troop ship. I cried when we boarded the Monterey, *despite the band's cheery welcome with* San Francisco, Here I Come.

I leaned on the rail and my ring caught the sunlight. I made a wish on it. I hung onto the rail, watching the horizon fade. A GI passed by and told me not to cry. But it was not until I met my old friend Ulla in the corridor that led to our cabin, #119, that I was able to dry my tears—what a surprise!

A lifetime has passed since that memorable voyage. I have so much for which to be thankful. Words fall short. I have enjoyed a rich gathering, with many gains and losses, but never without hope. And as for my youthful question about the existence of God, yes, I know he's out there. And I remain—a swimmer on a rocky raft.

SANTO TOMÁS SHANTY
Front Row: Don, Jim, Doreen, Maria holding Skippy, Bert.
Back Row: Friends.
(Photo imperfections due to damage to the camera)

CPSIA information can be obtained
at www.ICGtesting.com
Printed in the USA
FSOW04n1651120216
16886FS